Frances Tenenbaum, Series Editor

HOUGHTON MIFFLIN COMPANY
Boston • New York 1999

Small Gardens

How to get the most impact from the least space

GLENN MORRIS

TO ELIZABETH LEE MORRIS

Taylor's Guide and *Taylor's Weekend Gardening Guides* are registered trademarks of
Houghton Mifflin Company.

Library of Congress Cataloging-in-Publication Data

Morris, Glenn, date.
    Small gardens : how to get the most impact from the least space / Glenn Morris.
      p. cm. — (Taylor's weekend gardening guides)
    Includes index.
    ISBN 0-395-86643-X
    1. Landscape gardening. I. Title. II. Series.
    SB473.M665   1999
    635.9 — dc21   98-27336
                                      CIP

Printed in the United States of America.

WCT 10 9 8 7 6 5 4 3 2 1

Book design by Deborah Fillion
Cover photograph by Steve Silk / *Fine Gardening*

CONTENTS

Contemporary gardening is bursting with creative trends. There is a renewed emphasis on perennial plantings and a greater sensitivity to self-sustaining landscapes. Many gardeners are discovering that native plants are splendid additions to the garden, and many more are finding ways to cultivate whimsy and personal expression alongside their favorite plants.

But at the same time, gardeners are facing the reality that gardens are shrinking. Just as there are fewer cornflakes in a box and a pound of coffee is only 11.5 ounces, the residential garden is downsizing as well. While this may be merely a sign of the present time, it could also be a hint that pleasure gardening for the next generation of homeowners is going to be tight, folks.

This magical small garden transforms the limits of space into a limitless oasis. Small spaces offer one of gardening's grandest opportunities to astound and delight.

Small sites present landscaping challenges to both experienced and novice gardeners. Trying to shoehorn all of the traditional uses of a residential garden — circulation, contemplation, and cultivation, among others — into a smaller space is not an easy task. Many long-established design practices, such as using a gracious expanse of lawn as a centerpiece, do not seem to fit into the reduced scheme of things. Gardeners contemplating a small-space design must wrestle with this and other gardening assumptions. The past luxury of abundant suburban space makes anything less seem almost un-American.

Adding to the first-time gardener's problems is that small gardens are the "red-haired stepchildren" of the periodical publishing world. According to the expansive standards of home and lifestyle magazines, small gardens are not topical. They are not often featured, and when you do read about them, the examples either have the exquisite craftsmanship of a Fabergé egg, or are snappy and creative treatments of remnant spaces. The gardens are beautiful, but their appeal is narrow.

Even published "before and after" garden scenarios, no matter how effective, can help only so much with the bare-bones space allotted to a townhouse. Every gardener spends time puzzling about what to do and where to begin, but the problem just gets tougher as the space shrinks.

This book offers some basic assistance in designing gardens for small spaces. It offers a simple methodology for getting from the garden of your dreams (where everything is perfect) to the garden of the real world (where everything is perfect but you have to plant and maintain it all). The effort you put into designing your garden will yield a haven more satisfying than one built by successive bursts of spontaneous creativity and will save you time, money, and extraneous work. The downside of planning is that it is an unfamiliar task that can be slightly tedious.

Mark Twain once wrote to a friend that "if I had more time, I would have written a shorter letter." Like writing succinctly, gardening in small spaces offers a bigger challenge than a larger landscape does. Paradoxically, it may require a lot of attention yet can take a lot less time. To make a small garden both functional and lovely requires a different approach. As one wag noted, there's a lot more to a small garden than planting dwarf shrubs and shrinking violets.

Fortunately, it is a lot of fun, too.

Three perennials pack a punch against a fence. Pink centranthus billows before the spires of Siberian iris (back) and foxglove.

CHAPTER 1

THE SMALL-SPACE GARDEN

Two qualities set small gardens apart. The first is size, even though there's lots of room to quibble about how little small is, so to speak. The second is that the garden (or the space where you want to create one) is self-contained. If you stepped into it with a camera, you'd find that one photograph would give a fairly complete picture of the entire space. (Of course, a single photo couldn't do justice to your gardening efforts.)

Regardless of its shape, a small garden feels like a single unit in the same way an individual room in your house does. In most cases you can see what you have to work with as you move around the perimeter. If the phrase "What you see is what you get" or "Is this all?" come to mind, you are in small-garden territory.

There is no consensus about the number of square feet that categorize a garden as large, medium, or small. Obviously a 10-by-15-foot space is a small setting for either a garden or a garden party. For a townhouse site a 20-by-25-foot space, approximately the size of two standard parking spaces, is not unusual.

Use container plants to provide seasonal foliage and soften areas where on-grade planters are not practical.

Most often, the true measure of garden space is not made with a measuring tape but with a rule of thumb — if it looks and feels small to you, then it is. Behind this perception is the realization that the size of the site restricts your choices. If you must repeatedly make either/or decisions about what you can do in the space, it is definitely small.

WALLS 'R' US

Even a garden that allows some leeway can feel small, particularly if it is enclosed. Walls make the physical limits of a garden unmistakable; the space becomes as finite as a clay pot. This containment is an asset in that it defines the garden: there is no ambiguity about the garden edges. At the same time, however, walls introduce another design issue. Every object that you bring into the space to make it more usable also makes it seem smaller still. Ordinary garden furniture seems larger in a contained space. Call it the "Christmas tree effect" — when you bring indoors the tree you bought outside, the room shrinks.

Enclosed gardens also feel small because the walls restrict the view and therefore the perception of distance. The higher the wall, the more restricted the view, and the smaller the garden feels, regardless of its dimensions.

But one can find notable, magnificent exceptions to these generalities in cities as different as Charleston and Santa Fe. In each, the traditional walled courtyards not only enclose substantial spaces, but they also make adroit use of views and vistas beyond. The space feels bigger because "out-of-garden" features expand one's perception of the domain. Unfortunately, few new properties with walled sites are able to visually kidnap part of the horizon.

SMALL GARDENS WITHIN A LARGER PROPERTY

As contemporary builders wedge 4,000 square feet of house and driveway onto a 6,000-square-foot lot, they create many small, odd spaces. Each of these isolated nooks and corners is a potential garden within the larger landscape. Awkward sites can shine when treated as a unique, focused garden. The side yard

A larger courtyard can be a lush, intimate setting when enclosed by flowering evergreens such as the Indica hybrid azaleas in this Charleston garden.

between two single-family homes is an example, as is a space between the entry walk, the house, and the drive.

It is also possible to create a garden within a garden by framing the space with a hedge or a decorative fence. Many traditional kitchen or theme gardens are initially defined in this matter.

SIZE AND HORTICULTURAL CONDITIONS

A large suburban yard is likely to have pockets of sun, partial sun, and shade. One side of the property may be buffeted by winter winds while another basks in a mini-sauna of reflected low-angle sun. But it is rare to find these extremes together in small gardens, which tend to be more horticulturally uniform.

The size of the space does not change the sunlight, topography, and rainfall that determine gardening conditions. However, the amount of variation in natural conditions is minimized in a small garden. Curiously, the growing conditions may seem at odds with those in the surrounding "horticultural neighborhood."

It is not unusual for small gardens to have their own microclimates, with growing conditions that are significantly different from those a few yards away. A microclimate can be the equivalent of one hardiness zone warmer or colder than the local macroclimate. That's a large difference.

Microclimates generally develop in areas adjacent to a building and/or enclosed by fences or walls. These architectural features modify the neighborhood climate in several ways. Wherever south-facing building walls or garden fences reflect sunlight onto the earth, the soil temperature is likely to be higher close to the wall. This microclimate effect means that the area may be too hot for some plants in summer, yet warm enough in winter for plants that are generally not locally cold hardy.

Walls that serve as windbreaks from winter winds can change conditions at a site dramatically. Plant species that are marginally hardy in the region may survive because the wall thwarts the desiccating effects of wind chill.

A stepside site need not be a garden stepchild. Here are two floral solutions to such awkward places. Coreopsis, tall zinnias, and salvia festoon a concrete stair (facing page, top), while a flowering bouquet (bottom) covers a slope that is too steep to mow safely.

The north side of a building or wall acts as a shield from the sun longer through the year, resulting in a cooler-than-average environment. This effect is much more pronounced in gardens in the South.

Be aware of the advantages of a microclimate; try growing a tender plant or two in a spot that is sheltered from winter wind, where the soil is warmed by the heat of the house (or the clothes dryer vent). The satisfaction is in the growing.

NO ROOM FOR EXCESS WATER

Plants need water, of course, but they need the right amount given in the right way. Don't let your roof do the watering — runoff may double the amount of rainfall the garden gets. A surge of rainwater (or snow and ice) crashing from an unguttered roof in a downpour can crush foliage, wash soil away from the roots of plants, and saturate the soil, creating conditions favorable for diseases. The solution is to gutter the roof and install drain pipe to collect the water and route it away from the planting beds.

If the roof is already guttered, use perforated plastic pipe to carry the discharge away from the planting beds. If it is not possible to bury the pipe or otherwise hide it, use small stones to fill a trench beneath the downspout to carry the water away from your plantings.

TOPOGRAPHY

Topography means the lay of the land, including any noticeable natural features such as streams or rock formations. If the topography is difficult, the size of your site may limit the options for altering it easily and inexpensively.

A sloping site is the most common and annoying problem in a small garden. If the ground falls so much that a soccer ball will not stay put, it should be leveled. (No one enjoys trying to place a glass of iced tea on a sloping patio table.)

Fortunately, a slope is not a problem in a planting bed if it is constructed to retain the soil; apply mulch or plant ground cover to prevent soil from washing out of the beds during normal rains or watering.

Curving rock walls create simple terraces filled with lavender and lamb's-ears, making a feature of a small slope.

Gardening on the Level

It takes planning and work to turn a naturally sloping site to advantage. You create level ground either by filling in places that are too low or by cutting the earth out of areas that are too high.

Removing earth usually gives the best results because the soil you reveal is settled and compacted. If cutting back creates steep sides, you can face them with stone or timbers to retain the soil in place. Steep cuts may also be rounded or gently sculpted to provide a smoother look.

If you are filling a low area you may need to build a retaining structure to hold the new earth in place. Retaining walls can be made of precast masonry, stone, or rot-resistant pressure-treated timbers.

When filling, you first frame the shape and height of the raised surface. Then you bring in the fill material, tamping it, either by rolling a weighted drum or renting a mechanical tamper, to create a solid surface.

Changes in elevation make for small-garden drama. Above, tall evergreen rhododendrons frame a stepped path.

Stepped or Terraced Gardens

You can create very dramatic and attractive gardens by modifying steeply sloping sites with a series of landings or terraces connected by steps. Terraced or stepped gardens are visually enticing because of the different heights and the drama of looking up or down into plantings.

The art of terracing is to provide attractive, sure footing under all weather conditions. The steps should allow one to climb or descend with a natural stride, and there should not be so many steps that the climb is exhausting. The terraces should be comfortable, attractive interludes along the way.

Consider hiring a landscape professional or builder to help you design a safe, functional sequence of steps and terraces. A professional will be aware of local building code requirements for steps and will be able to suggest innovations such as adjoining planters and night lighting.

Express yourself! The cheery, sprightly greeting of these cosmos would make a grinch smile.

Chapter 2

How Size Influences Garden Design

The size of the space affects your choices of plants and other garden objects. Since you are likely to see everything in the garden at once and at close quarters, it becomes important to have the plants, furnishings, and accessories visually compatible.

Every plant and object should nudge the garden along toward a chosen theme. Mix and match, but avoid mismatch. Think in terms of building visual harmony when selecting plants and garden furnishings. The whole business is akin to dressing for a cocktail party, where dress, shoes, and jewelry all work together to create an ensemble suitable for the occasion.

Small gardens are similarly composed ensembles. You pick the pieces of the garden wardrobe you prefer and blend them to make a special place dressed for your use, which is the primary occasion. There is some method to the process, but it is not clinical; it's personal and hands-on.

Small gardens should be neat, like this buoyant courtyard. Eliminating lawn care frees up time for more expressive gardening.

The Need for Focus

Small gardens are most effective if they are organized around one dominant theme, use, or object. Such a theme or use might be a small table and chairs for outdoor dining, or it might be a rustic bench used for occasional sitting or a sundial or small water feature in a contemplative setting. Whatever your particular need and use for the garden, try to focus on that purpose and orchestrate the rest of the space to support it. A deliberately focused garden imparts its purpose clearly and looks better for this.

Designing to Scale

Smaller spaces affect your perception of objects. An average-sized purple-leaf plum or flowering dogwood, which acts as an accent tree in a spacious suburban landscape, looms as big as a sequoia in a small garden. Similarly, a table that seats four can seem oversized only because of the smaller frame of reference. Expect the intimacy of a small space to alter proportion by making average-sized plants and objects seem larger.

Under the Magnifying Glass

The proximity of everything in a small setting is a mixed blessing. Exquisite details are certainly more easily seen and appreciated, as is fragrance, but so are the unruly edges. The more you see, the more you see to improve.

Because every detail is highly visible, it is important to be meticulous about craftsmanship, selection of materials, and routine maintenance. If you are building a small arbor or bench, buy the best possible grade of wood. The increase in cost will be easily offset by long-term satisfaction in appearance and longevity.

Stay on top of mulching and weeding, especially when a garden is young and the plants have not yet grown together. A garden that appears well tended communicates care and attention, regardless of the size of the plants.

Delicious in their detail, interesting, well-maintained plantings convert a straight-shot walk into an intriguing stroll.

MEASURE MAINTENANCE IN MINUTES

A big plus of small gardens is that they are quicker and easier to maintain than suburban landscapes. This is a true economy of space: there are fewer leaves to rake and smaller beds to weed, mulch, and edge.

Plan your garden with the notion of making maintenance a quick, easy grooming instead of weekly warfare. Begin by reducing the number of repetitive chores it takes to keep the garden going. Mowing the lawn is the most repetitive garden task; edging is a close second. If you plant a turf-free garden, you eliminate one task altogether and substantially reduce the other. Not only do you free up the minimum of one and a half to three hours a week necessary for lawn care, but you eliminate the need for equipment storage as well. Enticing, isn't it?

With thoughtful design and plant selection, maintenance can be reduced to little more than removing unwanted debris, watering, grooming plants and beds, and feeding and mulching annually. Spread these tasks over the gardening year, and the word "chore" hardly applies.

Why not create a garden that doesn't require power tools for maintainence? There's a reachable goal that will make a small garden the loveliest of joys.

A PLACE FOR PERSONALITY

Once, after looking over a garden feature in a national periodical, an older gardener with a natural flair for place-making offered a gentle critique. "There's no serenity there," she chided, pointing to an effusive display of horticultural showmanship. Her point was that you couldn't see the garden for the flower collection. It was a nice reminder that flowers alone don't make a garden; it's how you fit flowers and other features together that makes it effective.

Her remark is also a reminder that all gardens are personal. Small gardens, however, display your personality more readily. If you have room for only a few things, choose your personal favorites and arrange them in every nook and cranny. Gardening small cleverly distills what you really think, feel, and want to express. It reveals the essential horticultural you.

A small garden gives you permission to do whatever you want, such as growing fresh tomatoes or sugar snap peas in the middle of the flowers. If you like it, grow it. It's your garden to enjoy.

This circular brick pathway unifies the plants in the center with those outside.
The smaller size of the plants keeps them from overwhelming the space.

CHAPTER 3
DESIGNING SMALL-SPACE GARDENS

Garden design is a combination of puzzle solving and exterior decorating. The puzzle part involves figuring out what pieces you need and how best to arrange them to make the garden work for you. The exterior decorating is polishing the design to the point that it will give you perpetual delight.

The process of designing involves making lots of little decisions about how to modify the site to make it useful for your needs and as attractive as possible. It is just like furnishing a room except that in a garden some of the "accessories" change with the seasons and the years. Some rooms in a house are more demanding than others, and so are some gardens. Some designs just fall into place; others take weeks of mulling and scheming to work out.

The more you can be involved with the design of your garden, the greater your pleasure as the plants grow and the garden fills and becomes the comfort zone you intended.

DECIDE ON THE PURPOSE

How will you use the garden? As a quiet retreat for reading the paper or entertaining? Will it be a spot to grow flowers, herbs, tomatoes? Will it be a backdrop for an interior room? Understanding your purpose is the first step in deciding what you will need in the garden and where it should best go.

The concentration of color in a small space has high landscape value. Why plant two shrubs when more flowers can do the job better?

The location of your site can be an important guide to making it as functional as possible without undue expense. The theory here is to take what the garden site offers and improve upon the givens rather than refashioning it altogether. Consider the following ideas.

- Most front garden sites are too public for quiet retreats.
- A site that is already partially private or is easily enclosed may be best for outdoor entertaining.
- A narrow side yard is a natural passageway, or it can be developed as a contemplative garden.
- Sites that get full or partial sun have the most potential for growing flowers.
- Woodsy backdrops are excellent for attracting birds.

Think of the activities you want to do in your garden as your outdoor agenda. Unless your small-space garden will be entirely for pleasurable viewing, you'll have to decide what physical objects or garden elements you need to make the place work as you intend.

- Make a list of likely outdoor activities, such as flower gardening, entertaining, and relaxing. These are an important part of the program. The activities you do the most probably require the greatest space. What are your priorities?
- Sit in the middle of the site and imagine what you want to see in each direction. Imagining the location of flower beds or a bench is the purest form of design. What you imagine can be even more important to the final design than the activities you are considering.
- How visible is the garden from the house? A garden easily seen from inside is a continuation of your living space. Accordingly, it should be a landscape that beckons in all seasons.
- Do you want to attract wildlife or grow specialty plants such as climbing vines or roses? In these cases, the plants' horticultural requirements and the environmental aspects of the site should drive the design.
- Clip pictures from garden magazines. This is wonderfully liberating — there's no patent on good garden ideas. When you see something you like, research it to see if it is adaptable to your site and horticultural zone.

A low evergreen hedge frames the flowers in this front yard and provides the garden's "bones" during the dormant season.

Seeking Design Help

Hiring a landscape professional to help you design your garden is strictly a matter of personal comfort. Most simple landscape designs do not require professional assistance, but that doesn't mean you wouldn't benefit from a design consultation. A landscape professional will have design expertise as well as a knowledge of similar gardening challenges. He or she can offer specialized local knowledge about plants and construction and help you avoid trouble spots you may not know about.

If you have ambitious ideas, such as a deck, an arbor, or a patio, consider getting some professional assistance if for no other reason than to review your ideas for soundness.

If you feel your design is not going anywhere, you can almost always find a professional design consultant whom you can hire for an hour or more. Such an investment will provide great rewards in ideas and rekindle the creative flame.

WALKS, PATIOS, AND PRIVACY

Wrestling your ideas into a manageable design is the next big task. With a good idea of how you want to use your garden, it's time to play with arrangements of space to see what works.

If walks, sitting areas, or privacy elements are a part of your garden program, start by allocating space for these features. These important and sometimes costly elements merit focused planning since they may require special construction or design assistance. Give these three components top priority for location, material, and shape, by working in the following order. First connect the dots (route the walkways), then spread the welcome mat (create a sitting area), then wrap the package (delineate or enclose the garden).

Walkways are the first concern because they are used more than any other element. Route them exactly where you want people to go. The most obvious routes are from a door to a garden gate or from a parking area to an entry. Use this transportation spine as a physical and visual link to other garden elements, such as patios and planting areas. Walks used daily must have an attractive all-weather surface. Less frequently traveled walks can be steppingstones or graveled paths.

Entertaining or just sitting outside is easier and more enjoyable on a level, solid surface, whether it is decking or pavement. After you have located the walkways, plan for an attractive surface for tables and chairs, perhaps a masonry patio or a deck with built-in benches. This will become a visually important feature in the garden design.

Providing a measure of privacy brings a sense of comfort to any garden space. The adage "Good fences make good neighbors" is never more true than between adjoining gardens in townhouse communities. True privacy is best achieved with a solid wall or fence. However, you can achieve a feeling of separation and make a garden space comfortable simply with planting.

Walks are very important, and they need not be dull. This townhouse garden (facing page, top) derives its visual appeal from the arrangement of the walkways, which create interesting spaces. The strong geometry of this sunny sitting area (facing page, bottom) with plantings of vegetables and herbs gives it a slightly formal air.

Framing the Garden

Framing is using plantings or architecture to define a space or create an enclosure.

Framing with structures

Fences and walls immediately secure the garden visually and physically and need less than a foot of precious garden width to do the job. They also serve as backdrops for plantings, provide support for decorative items, and can be marvelously interesting when planted with vines.

However, fences and walls may be expensive to construct and may be restricted in height and location by zoning regulations. They also may limit access to the house and other parts of the grounds.

Framing with plants

Plants offer the advantages of variety and economy. Evergreen plants can screen unwanted views and be a backdrop for the garden composition. Using evergreen and deciduous plants together offers less privacy but more horticultural interest. Some plants can be sheared into a hedge, which gives the effect of a fence.

The disadvantages of plants for framing are that they take up more space than a fence and usually take longer to become effective. Also, plants need water and feeding and may be injured or die.

SKETCHING GARDEN IDEAS

On a piece of graph paper, first rough out the shape of the garden, then make several photocopies of the sketched diagram. On one of the photocopies, draw in the walkways, then add the sitting areas that you want. Try out various ideas on the photocopies. Make the shapes interesting, try turning them different ways — aligned at an angle instead of squared up to the building lines. Be wild and free with your sketches. Plan to make a lot of sketches (it's always easier to erase pencil than to remove concrete) until you find a combination of shapes that is appealing. Try not to worry about what is "right" or "good" design; the important goal is that the design works for you and is right for your site. Follow the Shakespearean line — *As You Like It*.

Usually by this stage of the design, methodology starts to fly apart. This is the time when garden design asserts its organic nature, as one idea erupts unexpectedly from another, which cues something else, and so on. It's great energy, but it can be hard to rein it in and stay focused.

The bold use of color, foliage size and texture, and plant form turns a narrow side-yard entrance into a lovely approach.

Let your ideas rest for a day or so, then begin to refine them by reviewing the site from every vantage point, starting with the one you'll use the most. Imagine what elements you would like to see from that spot: is it the walk or the patio, a special tree or water feature, or an exuberant display of flowers?

Refining a design is nothing more than tweaking it to make it look better. Take the rough sketches and make little adjustments to improve them: curve a walk slightly for interest, reconfigure a patio to provide planting space, relocate a planting area to make it visible from the house.

The focal point of this artfully constructed sitting area is a spectacular espalier. The space, barely 9 feet wide, is well used.

Although every garden and every gardener is unique, some basic principles and techniques have been so successful for so long that it's hard to argue against them. These tricks of the trade work regardless of a garden's purpose or style.

- **Keep the design simple.** Rely on basic geometry (squares, rectangles, circles) for the shapes of features such as patios, walks, planting beds or water features.

- **Divide by three**. In our culture, thirds are more interesting than halves, so think in threes when partitioning your space. The "rule of thirds" makes a space dynamic instead of predictable and creates more freedom to diverge from symmetry. Rather than plunking a tree down smack in the middle of a bed, plant it to one side, leaving the remaining two-thirds of the bed for other plants.

Heron statues are used as an accent in a garden corner. These stand in a bed of strawberry geraniums and fallen camellia blossoms. The backdrop plant is Japanese fatsia.

- **Be consistent in theme.** Choose garden elements and plants to reinforce the theme of your garden. A Japanese rock garden probably should not have terra-cotta wall ornaments or Mexican tiles. By following a single theme, you will avoid a hodgepodge look.

- **Be consistent in style.** Use formal materials in formal settings and casual materials where a relaxed atmosphere is desired. Sticking with a single style and tone increases the unified feeling of the garden.

- **Be bold.** Contrast generates visual interest. Make any changes in shape or form bold enough to show your intent. This is the difference between designing a curve and leaving a wiggle.

- **Use accents carefully and sparingly.** Accents, such as unusual plants or garden objects, are points of visual interest that draw your attention. An accent must be more eye-catching than its backdrop and located for emphasis. Too many accents makes for a busy, disjointed look.

- **Don't mix and match materials.** Using several different building materials or styles of construction creates clutter. Pick a paving style and a fence style and stick with them. If you must change paving materials, do so when you change elevations (stepping off a deck onto a path) or at transitions, such as gates.

GIVING THE GARDEN A HEART

All gardens benefit from having a central feature. This keeps the design simple, focused, and plays to our natural comfort with organized space. It creates a more serene setting than one in which several elements compete for center stage.

When reviewing the design, make certain that one feature is the most visually important item. It might be a statue, a trellis, or a beautiful small tree. Whatever it is, it should set the tone without detracting from the garden's purpose.

For example, a patio that is key to how you will use the garden may seem too ordinary to be a focal point. But a fountain on the far side of the patio provides a handsome focus that increases the garden's appeal without changing the primary use. Similarly, artful planting, rock work, or statuary in the beds adjoining a walkway downplays the visual importance of the walk but establishes the mood of a garden passage.

Some items have more eye appeal than others in this regard. Keeping the purpose of the garden foremost in mind, see if the addition of one of the following items will provide the visual anchor that unifies the garden space.

- A water feature, particularly one with moving or bubbling water, is hard to surpass for allure. The mystique of water resonates with our cultural notion of the garden as an oasis. Water features can be as simple as a handsome "plug-in" fountain or complex enough to require professional installation. Without doubt, a water feature elevates a garden more than any other element can.

A garden with a heart is a comfortable place. Above, a bench at the end of a walk is the focus. Below, a sundial is the centerpiece; low-growing lamb's-ears inch across the brick pavers.

- An architectural element such as a pergola or a trellis can be visually power-ful. These features are symbolic of shelter, and the eye naturally seeks them out wherever they are placed. When covered with flowering vines, a pergola or trellis can be a garden tour de force.

- An object such as a bench or statue at the end of a walk or path gains impor-tance because of its placement. It becomes a visual terminus or destination.

- A framed feature, such as a small patch of lawn with a wooden border or a ground cover surrounded by a clipped hedge or brick edge, can be a very hand-some focus.

- A centerpiece, such as a sundial or statue, that intentionally encroaches on a walk is visually important because you cannot ignore it. Plants that spill over a walk, however, should attract attention without creating a hazard.

- Displaying an object at a height above the walking surface will give it greater importance. Placing a statue on a pedestal or planting an ornamental tree in a raised bed or planter will add the emphasis of height to a central feature.

- The eye naturally jumps to light or bright colors. Thus a white or a light-colored plaque or bas relief on a wall immediately attracts attention.

PUTTING MEASUREMENTS TO IDEAS

The more things you want to do in the garden, the smaller the space seems. It is one thing to know you want a patio, another to know how big it should be. The same is true with space for trees, planters, and walks. Here are some com-mon garden components and suggested dimensions for them. You may have to fudge these suggestions some to fit your site, but these will work.

Walks

- Walks for casual use may be made of pavers or set stones about 16 inches wide. Steppingstones in turf between beds should be "mower wide."

- Garden paths of gravel or stepping stones may be 12 to 16 inches wide. The stones should be spaced to the length of a stride.

Old millstones and coarse flagstones make a handsome primary walkway.

Do You Need a Plan?

It is a good idea to have detailed, dimensioned plans drawn by a draftsman or landscape design professional if you want a landscape contractor to build walks, patios, walls, or fences. A sketch plan with accurate measurements scaled on graph paper may be all that a contractor will need to give you a construction estimate or that you will need to estimate amounts of materials to purchase.

Detailed plans are not necessary for most small do-it-yourself gardens. It is much faster to lay out design ideas on the ground, using a garden hose to define the shapes of walks and planting areas. This method gives you a chance to look at different layouts quickly and easily. Once you find the shapes you like, mark them more permanently with stakes and twine or landscape paint as construction guides.

- Requirements for entry and service walks are usually covered by building codes. They should be direct, smooth (for wheeled items), durable, and no less than 3 feet wide.

- A walk at the base of a wall or fence should be at least 4 feet wide. (A 3-foot walk with a 16-inch planter at the base of the fence or wall is more attractive.)

- Walks that include space for benches or chairs should be about 6 feet wide, though a narrow bench or a chair that is not fully on the walkway will need less width.

Patios/Entertainment Areas

A good patio or deck design separates the sitting area from walking areas. There should be enough room to push chairs back from table.

- Two outdoor chairs at right angles need a 6-by-6-foot space.

- A table for two can tuck into a 5-by-5-foot space.

- A 30-inch-diameter table with four chairs needs an 8-by-8-foot space.

- A 48-inch table with four chairs takes a 10-by-10-foot space.

Planting Beds

Planting beds must provide space for roots to feed and crowns to spread. Plants can live in small containers, but undersized beds retard plant growth and invite health problems.

Note that plants will send roots under porous pavement such as brick-on-sand walks or patios. Eventually the roots may heave the surface, but the damage is easily repaired.

- Perimeter beds for most perennials and ground covers should be a *minimum* of 16 inches wide and have at least 16 inches of soil depth. Annuals can live in smaller beds.

- Perimeter beds at the base of a wall should be 18 inches wide because of the underground concrete footings.

- Planting sites for shrubs smaller than 6 feet should be at least 30 inches wide.

- Planting sites for taller shrubs should be at least 4 feet by 4 feet.

- Small shade trees need between 64 and 100 square feet of feeding area, that is, between 8 by 8 feet and 10 by 10 feet.

Other Garden Elements

- A portable grill needs about 5 feet by 3 feet of space, depending on whether or not the top flips back.
- A free-standing trellis to shelter a bench will take up about 8 feet by 6 feet on the ground, including posts.
- Smaller arbors to frame a walkway need 4 feet between posts and approximately 7 feet of overhead clearance.

CONSTRUCTION PRIORITIES

Sometimes building the garden's "bones," the permanent elements that give it shape and make it usable, must be accomplished over time, as money permits. It is usually better to take longer and do the garden well than to compromise on materials or construction in order to finish more quickly.

Here are some thoughts on staging the construction of a garden. (Gardeners always find money to purchase plants.)

- First, build important walkways and hard-surface areas, such as patios and decks. This immediately makes the garden usable.
- Second, establish the garden framework. A good-looking ornamental fence will help make the garden a room. If you can afford it, build walls at the same time as walkways and patios to economize on labor and deliveries.
- Third, install key or strategic plants. These include plantings that create the frame, provide privacy, or screen an undesirable object. A tree that is a central feature should be one of the first things into the ground.
- Furnish the garden with accessories. If dollars are tight, postpone buying statuary, a trellis, and benches unless they are critical to the garden design concept.
- Plant the remainder of the garden.

CHAPTER 4

TYPICAL SMALL-GARDEN SCENARIOS

The ideas and experiences of other gardeners provide a rich vein to mine for help with your own garden design. A peek at the creativity others have poured into settings like yours will stir up the idea pot. You will notice that the same problems are solved over and over again, but in different ways.

The four small-garden scenarios that follow embrace common circumstances. You are likely to identify with some aspect of one or more of these settings. Each scenario has a brief description followed by some thoughts on suggested uses, common design problems, possible solutions, key plantings, and things to note.

By solving the inherent design challenges, you are well on the way to creating a usable and beautiful garden.

TOWNHOUSE GARDENS

If you live in a new townhouse, the only potential garden sites are the space in front of the unit and the space at the rear. Both are likely to be nearly square. (End or corner townhouses may own additional space for a garden along one side.)

A sinuous path of steppingstones amid hosta, ferns, and astilbe turns a side yard into a shade garden.

New townhouses tend to be built as a series of side-by-side similar units, each with a smattering of "landscaping." The front garden site, facing the street, is as wide as the townhouse and includes the land from the building wall to any public sidewalk. It may or may not include a shade tree planted by the builder, but it certainly will have some evergreen shrubbery across the foundation. Paved entry walks and landings or porches reduce the plantable garden space.

Rear garden sites will also be as wide as the unit but the depth may vary, particularly if residential parking is located behind the townhouse. The heating/cooling units servicing the residence are usually in the rear. A townhouse unit with a garage has even less available garden space because of the driveway serving the garage.

Possible Uses

The public setting and the walkway mean that the front of a townhouse is best used as an entry garden or flower garden. The rear space can serve different uses, among them outdoor entertaining, recreational gardening, or as a private retreat.

Common Design Problems

- Townhouse garden sites often are not well defined. Your allotted space may simply run into the site next door with no visual distinction between them.
- There is frequently an inherited landscape consisting of evergreen shrubbery huddled at the foundation of the building and a patch of lawn.
- Rear gardens lack a clear sense of space and may have no privacy or sense of purpose.

Solutions

Create a sense of enclosure in a front garden site by clearly delineating the boundaries. These sites cry out for a picket or wrought-iron fence to serve as a neat

The lawn is gone and flowers rule in the front yard of a townhouse (facing page, top). An arbor defines the entry to the townhouse garden below, and a fence separates the public and private spaces.

ornamental frame to the garden. If fencing is not an option, rely on plantings (low shrubs or a small tree) along the perimeter to establish the feeling of enclosure. Such plantings help make the entry walk a short transition from public parking into a private place.

Provide a central feature, such as a miniature lawn, ground-cover bed, small ornamental tree, or statuary, as the visual focus of the newly defined space.

Rear gardens must be contained and separated from common space. With so little space to spare, fencing is the best and quickest way to provide a sense of privacy from neighboring units.

Key Plantings

- Identify your existing landscape plants and determine their expected mature size. Newly constructed homes will have some landscaping provided by the contractor; in most cases the only thought behind it is "green side goes up." Probably the plants are too close to the foundation and too large for the location. Plan to dig and relocate them to more suitable sites.

- Plant one or more small trees or tree-form shrubs as close to the sidewalk or street as possible. This will create a foreground for the garden, serve as faux gate posts, and enhance the feeling of enclosure. A 20-foot-wide garden has room for a pair of small ornamental trees.

- Use low shrubs (3 to 4 feet high) to establish the frame of the garden and a backdrop for flowers. The smaller spireas, evergreen hollies, or even ornamental grasses fit this bill.

- Genuinely consider whether a lawn is a good idea or not.

Things to Note

You need to allow access to utility meters.

Unless you own an end unit, you should allow space for transporting construction, planting, and maintenance items between the front and the rear garden. Before you make a purchase, think about how you will carry it to the site.

Be sure there is an exterior water spigot in both front and back; all new plantings will need regular watering.

A picket fence creates a sense of enclosure and separates the public space from the private garden in this urban townhouse setting.

Clematis climbing on a lattice screens the area underneath the stairs and deck of a townhouse, creating an effect like living wallpaper.

Special Circumstances

Expansionist townhouse gardeners will use the verge, the public space between the sidewalk and the curb. This 18- to 36-inch-wide space is "default" property; you must maintain it even though it is a public right of way. It provides a great opportunity to plant ornamental grasses and tough perennials.

Many townhouses have second-story decks. If possible, design the deck to include storage space which is always needed. The shaded ground-level area beneath it is not particularly useful for gardening and can be converted to an outdoor sitting area.

For walkways, various inexpensive paving options (brick pavers or precast paving blocks separated by wood dividers) are easy to install. Flagstone may also be used. Be sure the surfaces do not trap moisture or dirt against any siding.

SIDE-YARD GARDENS

A side-yard garden is the outdoor equivalent of a hallway, a little chute of space between the house and property line, joining the front and back yards. An indispensable walkway, it may provide access to service or utility meters on the side

of the house. The side yard may also be used (in a limited fashion) for storage, utility placement, and the routing of service lines.

Side yards are gardens on the skinny, since the space rarely exceeds 15 feet in total width (less than 10 feet in new housing) and is much longer. Usually the space is too pinched for any active use other than walking.

Common Design Problems

- The main challenge is maintaining a usable passage while creating an attractive garden space. The choice of paving materials and the layout of the walkway sets the tone.

- Unless there is a wall or fence along the property line, the boundary may not be clearly defined.

- It is difficult to make storage areas and utility spaces both secure and attractive.

An urban townhouse garden uses the borrowed vista of neighboring buildings as a backdrop.

Solutions

- The walkway is everything in a passageway garden. It should provide solid footing, but informal paving such as steppingstones, bricks on sand, or pea gravel will work. Routing the walk from one side to the other in a gentle "S" curve or with a right-angle offset will vary the width of the planting areas and increase the interest of the space.

- Use a fence (or vine-covered lattice) to define the space and to screen any storage. Gates at either end will look attractive from the front or rear garden while screening the passageway. Hedges or shrubbery are not recommended because they take too much room.

- An overhead arbor the length of the passageway is an ambitious yet unique way to define the space. It will also make the space uniformly shady.

Key Plantings

The open side of the passageway may receive full sun, while the roof eave may shade the sides adjacent to the house completely. Such conditions make plant selection and water management tricky.

- Look for a durable evergreen ground cover to provide visual unity, reduce maintenance, and be a foil for more ornamental plants, which you can plant in the ground cover.

- Take advantage of a wall or fence by planting flowering vines or vigorous climbers and training them to cover it.

- Locate any trees on the property-line side of a side-yard passageway. This will enhance the feeling of enclosure.

This side yard (facing page) has a garden feeling. Positioning the fence at the back of the wall keeps the space from seeming pinched. At right, the details of a great gate and handsome walkway dress up a narrow side yard.

Things to Note

Know the drainage pattern. The side yard may be the only route for storm-water runoff to move between the front and back of the residence. Do not block this drainage when creating a passageway garden.

Any gate in a passageway should be wide enough to permit access by emergency repair equipment.

Special Circumstances

Consider using the passageway for a specialty garden. A side yard can be ideal for a raised-bed vegetable garden or a cutting garden. If it is sunny plant tomatoes; if it is shady, create a fern glade.

A side-yard passageway also can be an elegant entryway. In an urban location, consider installing a small fountain. The sound of water will help you leave the outside world on the far side of the gate.

GARDEN CORNERS

Every garden has a "corner," a part of the larger landscape picture that is physically and visually separate from the rest of the space.

The area between an entry walk and the house or garage is a garden corner (sometimes the only one a townhouse offers), as is the actual corner formed where two walls join. In such a space a free-standing planting bed can be a magnificent solution, an island garden.

An older term, garden vignette, comes to mind, meaning a miniature composition within a larger landscape. Garden vignettes were intentionally created (sometimes without benefit of a naturally distinct space) as interludes, places where the eye comes to rest before finishing the garden tour. Garden corners can be a visual rest stop, and are they fun! If you've ever attended an indoor garden exhibition featuring show gardens by landscape professionals, then you have an excellent idea of how full and rich a garden corner (or small garden) can be.

The curving walk of this Charleston side yard shows how dressy a passageway can be.

Possible Uses

Almost by definition, garden corners are remnant spaces that don't have to be anything particular — these are the joy spaces. Use them for theme gardens or for the pleasure of creating a composition of form, texture, and color.

Common Design Problems

- Decide what you want this "play space" to be. Take your cue from the horticultural conditions and the location in relation to the house. If your garden corner is visible from inside, make sure it has year-round interest. If it is tucked out of sight, inject the element of surprise, such as a retreat in the middle of culinary herbs, a fern glade, or a cutting garden.

- A well-defined space usually benefits from a central feature.

- Garden corners tend to be static — leftover places waiting for something to happen. You'll have to create depth and motion to invigorate the design.

Solutions

- Look for an element such as statuary, a sundial, ornamental small tree, or birdbath to be the dominant feature. Think of something that will anchor the space after the growing season.

- Select a supporting cast of plants to fill in around the feature without taking over the design.

- Choose a single material, texture, or color to unify the design. This element may be as simple as a gravel walking surface or a vibrant ground cover or a uniform mulch.

- To keep the garden from becoming too static, route a small steppingstone path through it. This also gives the garden depth.

Lilies, coreopsis, and phlox spiff up the narrow space between a driveway and the property line (left).
A little garden corner is turned to advantage with a statue and perennial containers (facing page).

Key Plantings

- Any plant selected as the central feature should have a distinctive character — a slightly curved trunk or branching that looks windblown. Seek out asymmetrical plants instead of perfect specimens to help put motion into the design.

- Look for filamentous plants that move in light breezes. Plants that attract butterflies and hummingbirds also bring energy to a possibly static place.

- Locate some plants so that the foliage intrudes on the walkway. This loosens the lines of the planting and frees it from the frame.

Special Circumstances

Take advantage of the natural topography to turn a garden corner into a theme garden. An area with poor drainage might make a wonderful wetlands garden filled with indigenous plants that like wet feet. Similarly, an area with an exposed rock outcrop and thin soil might be perfect for plants that tolerate drought, such as succulents and grasses.

COURTYARD GARDENS

There is tremendous range in the shapes and sizes of courtyard sites. An urban parking space with access to a public street is one kind of courtyard; others are private backyard retreats. Charleston, South Carolina, is celebrated for its walled courtyard gardens in all sizes and configurations, which the owners have imaginatively personalized. The row houses of Philadelphia's Rittenhouse Square (and other northeastern urban neighborhoods) have always had courtyards.

Innovative housing developments that cluster detached single-family homes around common open space often provide walled courtyards for the homeowner's private use. The concept is appealing, regardless of the courtyard's size — what goes on behind the walls is the owner's joy and opportunity. I think a courtyard represents the zenith of small-space gardening — a box with a floral present inside, where a lot of things can happen. Successful courtyard design will respond to cues from the architecture to become a genuine outdoor room.

This lovely garden vignette composed around rustic chairs provides space for quiet contemplation.

Possible Uses

Courtyard sites are challenging because they are nearly always big enough to accommodate several uses. With privacy assured, they are natural places for entertaining small groups, or they can be serene retreats. A courtyard may serve the residence either as an entryway or as an optional path between the wings of a building.

In this Charleston courtyard a simple rectangle of lawn is framed by borders bursting with color. It is a personal and expressive setting.

This courtyard in Santa Fe serves as an entry. The plantings have the spare beauty and muted hues of the Southwest.

Common Design Problems

- The classic dilemma is how to allocate enough space for all the different activities.

- Courtyards teeter on the edge of the lawn question — that is, they are on the borderline in size for the usefulness and economy of grass. Evaluate the long-term maintenance issues and other options in deciding whether or not to have a lawn.

- Courtyards need a compelling visual center of interest that has appeal from within the house as well as from the garden.

- It is important to maintain access for maintenance or emergency machines.

- Even though courtyards are enclosed, you may need to do more to establish privacy from adjoining taller buildings.

Solutions

Approach courtyard design as a series of small practical problems to be solved. Set design priorities as follows. First, carefully route the everyday walkways: entry walks, service walks, and connecting paths to outdoor features. Next, determine how you wish to use the remaining space and mark what is needed to serve that use. Be sure to relate the shapes to the interior rooms of the house.

Review the design to be sure that the central feature is a visual focus from inside the house. A lighted feature will be a centerpiece even at night.

Key Plantings

- Determine whether the perimeter plantings should grow above the wall either to frame a desirable distant view or to provide additional privacy from tall adjoining properties.

- Courtyards are large enough to handle one and possibly two or more feature trees or tree-form shrubs. Choose plants that will develop a muscular branching structure, such as a Japanese maple or crape myrtle. Such trees are perfect for dramatic night lighting. Also, when you look through them, the sense of depth in the garden is enhanced.

- If possible, plant trees at least 4 to 6 feet away from any walls. This scheme introduces a curve in the border planting and emphasizes the perception of depth.

- Make room for plants that have fragrant flowers; perfume in a walled space can be intoxicating.

- Consider an evergreen ground cover or dark mulch to unify the garden.

- Vines, vines, and more vines. Never let a wall remain uncovered. Yes, some vines may chink away at wood and masonry, but they can be managed to minimize damage. If you like vines, plant them and let the estate lawyers worry about the damage.

Things to Note

A courtyard must have an interior drain to carry storm-water runoff away from the garden. Contact a landscape professional or building contractor if you are uncertain about the need for a drain on your property.

Even a large courtyard can succeed without a lawn. Here, raised beds billow with perennials that set off the gazebo.

Be sure there is an outdoor water spigot to serve the courtyard. It helps if there is room for the hose as well.

Bury a capped 1½-inch PVC pipe under any permanent walk that you build. These "empty" pipes are useful if you later decide to run electrical or irrigation lines from one side of the walk to the other.

Provide a double-wide gate or other access for emergencies or for moving large pieces of furniture into or out of the house.

Special Circumstances

In zero-lot-line properties the exterior of a windowless house wall (or in some cases a garage wall) is a courtyard garden wall for the neighboring residence. It's the neighbor's house, but it is your garden backdrop.

CHAPTER 5

DESIGNING WITH PLANTS

Creating a small-space design, selecting the plants, and arranging them in your garden is more art than engineering. The principles and rules of design can serve as guides, but the most rewarding path is to experiment. Recipes and formulas are helpful, but the final product tends to be better if you tinker with new ideas as the plan proceeds.

It is sure to happen that a little gardening success early on will generate ever-increasing enthusiasm. As your confidence soars, so does design audacity. Let it rip! Only the realities of horticulture, which determine what plants will thrive in your garden, should trump your creativity.

Still yearn for a simple formula to get you started? Try this: select plants that are known to be locally reliable for crucial positions in the garden design. This will establish a solid foundation.

After that, be adventuresome. Small-space planting should be fun. There's no heavy lifting; no one keeps score.

This chapter offers ways to look at plants as well as suggestions on combining them into a garden composition.

The constancy of evergreen plants, such as the boxwood of this clipped hedge, is important to the garden's year-round attractiveness. Select locally reliable plants for such key locations.

Working with Misplaced Plants

In both new and older gardens, a good plant can be in the wrong place for a new design scheme.

Doing the work of digging and relocating older woody plants is admirable, but it promises marginal success, a lengthy recovery, and anxiety about the plant's survival. Success depends on size and species, the season of relocation, and the follow-up care the relocated plant receives. The key question is whether the plant is worth the time and effort to move it.

If the plant is a rare or unusual specimen, such as a boxwood or a dwarf Japanese maple, then consider relocating it. If it is chest high or taller and worth moving, don't try to dig it yourself instead, hire an experienced landscape contractor to move it. Comparing the cost of relocating the old plant with the cost of replacing it will give a good frame of reference for the plant's worth. Landscape contractors will dig and relocate existing plants, but they will not guarantee their viability after the move.

Discard more common plants, such as azaleas, hollies, and yews, unless they are easily replanted. This recommendation may seem harsh, but the most direct way to move forward with a new garden design is to make a clean sweep of the planting beds.

SHRINK THE PLANTS AND THE PLANT LIST

Because of the way small spaces affect perception, it is a good idea to "downsize" your plant palette. Plan to use large shrubs as if they were trees, medium-sized shrubs as backdrop plantings, and large perennials as you would shrubs in a larger space. (Consider this adjustment "upscale" gardening.)

Be patient. You are starting to *grow* a garden, not *assemble* one. The prevailing mistake in gardening today is overplanting. This means two things: too many plants and plants that are too large for the space available. Gardens that look full when started will be overgrown in as little as three years. Double-check the expected mature size of shrubs and trees to make sure there is room in the garden to accommodate them. At the same time, inquire about the appropriate spacing between plants.

UTILITARIAN PLANTS FIRST

Choose the plants that have jobs to do in the garden first. These are usually trees and shrubs that must block an unwanted view or establish privacy, create shade, define a space, or frame the garden. Look for plants that will accomplish the assigned job before you worry about their aesthetic qualities.

Smaller plants have been carefully selected and planted to grow together in this garden. The rhododendron in the foreground shows that small size does not hinder effectiveness.

Perhaps you want the garden to be a tour de force of planting; in that case there is no need for a central feature other than a splendid specimen plant. Let your purchase reflect the importance of the plant's place in the garden. Gardeners who are willing to pay $500 for a small arbor or trellis do not always extend that generosity to the purchase of a specimen plant, but for the sake of the garden they should.

Pay particular attention to selecting locally hardy and reliable plants for key positions. Don't bet the garden on a marginally hardy or rare plant, regardless of its outstanding ornamental characteristics.

EVERGREEN OR DECIDUOUS?

Evergreen plants retain their foliage throughout the year (actually, the leaves do drop, but over an extended period, so the plant is never bare). The foliage of deciduous plants drops to the earth in — what else? — fall. Both types have their place in the small garden.

Evergreens are essential to the garden's bones, defining space, establishing privacy, creating enclosure, and becoming the garden backdrop. Far from being dullards, these plants offer much in their forms, foliage textures, colors, and even flowers and fruit. Their hallmark is constancy, holding the garden together during the dormant season.

Deciduous plants are natural mirrors of the calendar. The change in their appearance over the growing season is like a pulse beating to the yearly cycle. While most appealing when they are in flower, deciduous plants bring change to the garden, especially in fall, when their foliage may blaze with color before dropping. The price is a winter of gardening discontent, the leafless period some people find too barren to tolerate.

"Deciduous" is not an absolute term. A plant that drops its leaves in fall in one part of the country may not do so in a warmer climate. If you move to a warmer zone, you may find that some deciduous standbys have gone evergreen. (In Tampa, you can move your houseplants outside!) If you move, consult a local nurseryman for recommendations on reliably evergreen plants.

DESIGNING WITH FORM

One of the first things you notice about a plant is its shape — upright, rounded, clumping, spreading, filamentous, mounding, or matting. Form depends on the plant's natural branch or stem structure and its foliage. The form of a plant is an element of the garden throughout the year and this is an important design consideration. This is obviously true of evergreen trees, shrubs, and ground covers, but deciduous woody plants imprint their form on the garden as well. So, to some extent, do perennials, even though the foliage that gives them their form withers before winter.

A birdbath anchors this garden filled with a variety of contrasting colors and plant forms.

These cactuses create a study in dramatic plant forms. Juxtaposing plants with different forms is a fundamental way to create garden interest.

One of the simplest ways to create variety and interest in a garden is to select plants with different forms and place them next to each other. Such simple contrasts — a tall, twiggy plant such as heavenly bamboo *(Nandina domestica)* emerging from a planting of mounding dwarf willow-leaf cotoneaster *(Cotoneaster salicifolius repens)*, say — create a composition more interesting than the individual plants alone.

LOOKING AT FOLIAGE

The foliage of a plant is the muscle and flesh on the bones of the branches. Foliage establishes the basic colors and textures — the feel — of the garden.

The maroon foliage of a Japanese maple is used to accent a water feature. This is an adroit use of foliage color.

Foliage color means the typical, healthy color of the leaves during the growing season. In addition to the many different hues of green, leaves may be maroon, lime green, gold, or rose-tinted. Some needle-leaf conifers sport colors from bright gold to powder blue to deep blue-green. Many plants have varieties with variegated foliage, the leaves edged or blotched with cream, yellow, or a golden color. The perennial hostas or funkias are especially noteworthy for their variegated leaves.

Use foliage to provide long-term color in the garden. As an element of color, leaves are effective for a much longer season than flowers are. Plants with unusual foliage color jump to the forefront of the viewer's interest simply because the norm is green. Few plants have as much panache as a red-leaved Japanese maple, and variegated plants brighten darker spots of the garden.

Foliage color may also change seasonally. The new spring growth of evergreens is often a lime green surge along the stems. Fall brings every color, from vivid reds, yellows, and orange to deep purples, in deciduous plants. Some conifers turn deep burgundy in winter. Change in foliage color over the year is often overlooked, but it is a subtle, valuable element of surprise in the garden.

If all plants were the same shape, color, and size, then foliage texture would be the easiest way to distinguish among them. Foliage texture is determined by the shape and size of the leaves. Plants may be loosely categorized as having fine, medium, or coarse foliage texture.

Plants with leaves less than 1 inch in length are considered to have fine texture. They have a delicate appearance that is best appreciated at close quarters. The ground cover periwinkle is a good example. Always consider the effect of the entire plant. Many needle-leaf evergreens, such as junipers, meet the definition of fine texture in the strictest sense, but their form gives them a medium or coarse texture.

The leaves of coarse-textured plants are at least 4 inches long and approximately 2 inches wide or wider, easily visible from across a large garden. The hydrangeas, canna lilies, and flowering tobacco readily come to mind as representative plants.

Plants between these extremes, and there are many, have medium texture. Generally, plants with medium texture or with intricate foliage and delicate texture are the most desirable for a small garden. The finer detail fits the size of the space and the pace of movement typical of small confines.

Medium-textured plants, such as rhododendrons, can serve as backdrops for this delicate tableau. Using plants with different foliage textures, such as bearded iris and peonies, together is a great way to establish contrast and interest.

Plants that are attractive, bold, and eye-catching in a larger landscape may seem overpowering in the small garden and should be used carefully. Leatherleaf mahonia *(Mahonia bealei)* is a good example. This superbly architectural evergreen shrub has compound leaves and wide, spiny leaflets atop stout canes. It's a living exclamation point in a large shrubbery planting, but up close in a small garden, it can seem formidable, almost repelling. The similar but more subtle Oregon grape holly *(Mahonia aquifolium)* may be a better choice, depending on the size of the space.

The broad leaves of the water lilies, the lotus, and the tall canna lilies beyond give this water feature a lush tropical feeling.

WORKING WITH COLOR

Whether you use flowers as an accent or in a bountiful eruption of bloom, it is the use of color that gives a garden personality and mood. Floral color is one of the most appreciated aspects of plants. You may use it sparingly, favoring muted hues to create a landscape that is serene and subdued, or you may plant a rainbow's worth of color for a garden as brassy as a Sousa march.

The variety of flower color and form is staggering. Many flowering trees, shrubs, and vines, the staples of larger landscapes, are suitable for small garden spaces. The drawback to using them is that you risk concentrating the garden's bloom in a narrow time window.

Small gardens are made for the boundless world of the plants known as herbaceous (nonwoody) perennials, annuals, and bulbs — the plants we refer to offhandedly simply as flowers. These are the headliners in a small garden. When most of us think of a garden, it is flowers that color our imagination.

Using a Color Wheel

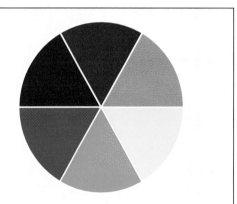

Many gardeners have a good eye for color, blending shades easily and masterfully. Other gardeners work by trial and error. Of course, no one will grade your efforts, but to save time, a simple color wheel is helpful, for it allows you to preview combinations.

A color wheel depicts the colors of the spectrum as equal-sized segments of a circle. The colors directly opposite each other on the wheel — red and green, yellow and purple, and so on — provide the strongest contrast. The effect of these colors side by side is vibrant, almost jarring. Colors that are adjacent on the color wheel tend to blend together very smoothly. Colors one third of the wheel removed from each other — red and yellow or yellow and blue, for example — naturally create bright, vivid displays that are not garish.

Red geraniums and red flowering salvia, with their green foliage, are as vivid as the wheel predicts, magnets of color in the garden. Tried-and-true flower combinations such as red and yellow tulips or yellow and blue pansies seem to be picked right off the wheel.

Soft yellow basket-of-gold and violet creeping phlox complement each other. Their mounding forms cascade over the face of a rock wall.

The broader issue of using color to establish a mood or create an effect is more important than the specific flowers you plant. The primary purpose of color is to create visual excitement. Placed against the universal green tones of foliage, color is an accent by definition. When there is color, you will automatically look at it, so make it worth the look!

Red, yellow, and orange are the colors of fire trucks and carnivals. The urgency and high-energy jubilation of these hues bring snap and pop into the garden. These are fire colors, and we think of them as warm, sometimes "hot," especially the reds and oranges. Strongly advancing colors, such as crimson red, hot pink, or red-orange, will always dominate a garden composition. Select these colors to rivet a viewer's eye or create a festive mood.

Shop for the Garden, Not for a Plant

The more engaged you are as a shopper for plants, the more satisfied you will be with what you bring home and put into the ground. As you select plants at the nursery, take the time to arrange them the way you intend to plant them in your garden. Even though they are in containers, you can still get a good idea of how their form, foliage, and color qualities will look next to each other.

Being able to examine your plant combinations before bringing them home is always satisfying. It is especially useful when selecting perennials and annuals that are in bloom.

When you have found a combination you like, confer with the garden center staff about the horticultural compatibility of the plants with the conditions of your site as well as about the recommended spacing between the plants for healthy growth.

Because the effect of bright colors is amplified in a small garden, you may want to consider turning down the wattage or interceding with a neutral hue. You might pick a less vibrant color or buy fewer plants of those that are especially vivid. Also, surround the hot colors with silver- or gray-leaved plants (lavender, lamb's-ears) to quiet them down a bit.

Curiously, warm and hot colors seem most natural when sunshine is bright and the sky is azure — summer in northern latitudes, early spring and fall in the South. These colors are also splendid against the earth tones of the Southwest.

Greens, blues, and violets are nature's antidote for the hard-charging colors above. These are the colors of far-away mountains, shade-drenched glades, and twilight places and times that are soothing and serene. These cool, distant, even passive colors can be used in the garden to create a feeling of spaciousness and tranquility — to make a small space seem bigger and, even in the South, cooler.

There are no hard and fast rules about warm and cool tones in the garden because flower colors vary so much. Roses can show warm red hues or much cooler reds. Pink can swing both hot, as in portulaca, and cool, as in the blossoms of flowering vinca. The pink of some crape myrtles crackles with heat, while other varieties are the soft pink of a flannel nightgown.

A display that relies on perennials, bulbs, or bedding annuals to provide vivid colors is rarely overpowering, because it is not so heavy-handed. The naturally muting effect of the foliage tempers the show.

The key is to experiment to find color combinations that create the effect that's pleasing to you. Color correction is just a garden spade away. Here are some suggestions on how to play with garden color.

- Use color for emphasis, perhaps to call attention to particular features or to an entryway. Use that emphatic color in only one location at a time during the growing season.

- In gardens with strong architecture or sculpture, you may prefer soft, quiet colors. These hues will not compete for attention.

- Repeating the same color in different locations provides a feeling of unity.

- The same color appearing at different heights in the garden creates visual movement.

- Select plants that flower at different times of the growing season.

- Use longer-blooming annuals to carry the floral display while shrubs and perennials are not in bloom. Don't overlook caladiums and coleus — in each of these you will find leaf colors that will blend with anything.

- Soft, work-anywhere colors, such as silver, bronze, and some pinks, will blend with all other colors and pull the garden together.

- Placing light colors — white or pastels — in dark corners is calming.

- Abundant foliage will naturally mute "clashing" colors. Daylilies and peonies are examples.

- Be careful with vivid reds. Stop signs, taillights, and warning signals are red. Your garden shouldn't be too alarming.

- Yellow puts bounce in the garden; it is always upbeat.

- Blue flowers bring the sky to ground level; white brings the clouds. That's why these flower colors always work.

The biggest challenge is choosing which flowers to plant. The number of possibilities boggles the mind. There are always more flowers to try than places for them to grow. Investigate what thrives in your area, and look for nearby sources for these plants. As you shop, you can assume that you won't find all the flowers that you could grow, but established garden centers always offer plants that *will* grow. Take the time to cultivate a relationship with an established nurseryman, visit public gardens, and walk around other neighborhoods to see what other gardeners are trying.

Experiment with different flowers and color combinations. Select plants that flower at different times of the year. In this era of expanding mail-order gardening, new flowers are a phone call away.

COMBINE FOR CONTRAST

Use your knowledge of form, foliage, and color to group plants for contrast, which creates visual interest. Select several plants of one species to be the filler in a bed and add another, contrasting plant as the accent. Strong contrast between plants emphasizes their individual characteristics.

- Use spreading plants in front of upright species.
- Punctuate fine-textured evergreen plantings with a broad-leaved deciduous plant.
- Front coarse-textured plants with fine-textured plants.
- If your plants have similar textures, vary the foliage color.
- Plant upright perennials, such as bulbs, in beds of ground cover.

OTHER EFFECTS OF PLANTS

Plants display their flowers in many ways. The different shapes of flowers and the ways they are arranged on the stem offer another opportunity to mix things up a bit and keep the border looking lively. Some plants have single flowers atop long stems, others have flat-topped clusters of tiny flowers, and still others bear tall plumes of color. You can have an all-white or all-blue garden and still have a wide range of wonderfully different shapes. In effect, you can scatter color throughout the garden by varying forms and heights.

Plan your garden for fragrance. Scent is the most subtle yet evocative effect you can slip into a garden and too often it slips in by the back door as a surprise. Select your plants so that at least one fragrant flower is in bloom throughout the season. Consider using shrubs with fragrant flowers (see page 107) to achieve this objective.

Don't forget about fruiting effects — berries can be beautiful. You may want to include some plants that follow their floral display with interesting fruit or seed capsules. The ornamental grasses are particularly exquisite this way.

Pink and red geraniums above white-flowered sweet alyssum are showy against the evergreen backdrop, a good use of contrast in an entry planting.

The Question of Lawn

Lawn grass, the most economical multipurpose ground cover for *large* spaces, is not so satisfactory for small settings. The equipment and care schedule are the same, but the quantities of materials are smaller. Ironically, a small lawn may require more attentiveness: although weekly maintenence will take less time, the lawn, seen close up, has to look its best all the time.

Evaluate your need for a lawn with these questions.

- What will I be doing in the garden that *requires* lawn grasses?
- Would a ground-cover planting work as well as a lawn?
- Do I have room to store the necessary maintenance equipment?
- Will I be content without a lawn?

CHAPTER 6

MATCHING PLANTS TO PARTICULAR PLACES

The best-laid garden plans may get sidetracked at the garden center when a one-plant shopping mission turns into three alternate purchases and a spontaneous new planting scheme. But switching plants in mid-design or redesigning at the garden center is not a problem as long as you match the plants with the sites they will occupy.

There must be common ground (pun intended) between the plants and the place. Study the site conditions, then ask the right questions about plants you like.

PLANT HARDINESS

A plant's survival in your garden depends on many factors, such as the orientation of the garden, prevailing winds, rainfall, amount of sunlight, and the plant's origin. It also depends on whether your garden mirrors the range of the local hardiness zone, as shown on the map on page 115.

The United States Department of Agriculture's hardiness zone rating system indicates the general tolerance of a species to the average winter tempera-

---

Sunflowers (Helianthus) *and zinnias, which like sunny, well-drained sites such as these terraces, brighten a porch. Terraces are often more intriguing than straightforward foundation gardens.*

tures in different parts of the country. The rating is based on how plants of that species fared in trials across the country. The zones range from 1, the coldest, to 11, the warmest. A plant that is hardy to Zone 6 will survive the average winter temperatures of that zone (between –10 and 0 degrees Fahrenheit). A plant that is hardy to Zone 7 (0 to 10 degrees Fahrenheit) is at risk in Zone 6.

The hardiness rating provides a starting point for your expectations. If you shop from catalogs, order plants with identical hardiness zone ratings. Ordering plants hardier than your zone is usually safe: if you live in Zone 6, most Zone 4 plants will work fine — but not the reverse.

Hardiness zone ratings do not indicate a plant's tolerance for severe summer heat, which can be as deadly as winter winds. You will get the best information on any plant at a local botanical garden, arboretum, or garden center or from an experienced gardener in the area. Also, if you don't see the plant growing locally, it may not grow well for you.

Site Alignment

The compass orientation of your garden is a factor in selecting plants. If the garden adjoins your house, the compass orientation is the direction you face with your back to the house. Here's generally what to expect.

North-facing gardens tend to be cooler than the average temperatures for your area. Since the low-angle winter sun rarely warms the soil directly, these gardens will have a delayed spring. In fact, the beds closest to the house may receive direct sun only in summer.

East-facing gardens have the best balance — bright morning sun without the severe direct rays of midday and afternoon. These conditions permit the widest range of plant selection within the winter hardiness limits.

South-facing gardens have milder winter conditions, but summers may be scorching. Sunlight reflected from the building into the garden rapidly raises the temperature around the plants and may permit you to grow more tender species.

Southwest- and west-facing gardens also must contend with severe heat and water evaporation, particularly in planting beds next to buildings. In the South, these gardens must be shaded for comfortable sitting.

This attractive garden corner uses a uniform foliage backdrop as the foil for white statuary and the hovering blossoms of columbine.

This colorful courtyard garden marries plants native to hot, dry deserts with those from seashore environments. The bright pink blooms of sea pinks are the colorful centerpiece.

HOURS OF SUNLIGHT

The preferred exposure of a plant is frequently described as either full sun, partial sun, or shade. It can also be a range such as sun to partial sun or partial sun to shade. If you can assess your garden in these terms, it will help you match plants and place.

Observe where, when, and for how long the sun shines in your garden during the summer, when the sun's rays are hottest. The time of day the sun strikes a garden makes a huge difference in its effect on plants.

- A garden that receives no shade or shadow all day or during midday (from approximately 10:30 A.M. to 3:30 P.M.) is a full-sun garden.

- The filtered light of a tree canopy is considered partial sun.

Hostas and ferns are excellent plants for shaded areas. Both look lush and require very little care after planting.

- Sun between dawn and 10:30 A.M. is all goodness for plants, whether they prefer full sun, partial sun, or partial shade.

- In the South, direct sun between 2:30 P.M. and sunset is harsh for partial-sun plants such as azaleas. North of Maryland, these hours of sun are less severe.

SIZING PLANTS UP

Always ask how tall and wide a plant is expected to grow, then ask yourself if you have that kind of room. Use the size of your planting beds and the proximity of walks or sitting areas to determine size limitations.

Oregano (left) and sage are easily contained in small planters. Planting in individual beds is an excellent way to control vigorous spreaders such as mints.

Seek plants that grow gradually to the size you need. Plants marketed as fast-growing often have weak stems or trunks — and they may grow much larger than you need.

Space plants in the bed according to their projected mature size. Proper spacing usually makes a garden look underplanted, but the "bare" space can be filled with annuals.

IS THIS PLANT TOO VIGOROUS?

Vigor and toughness are good, right? Not always. There are many gardeners who are wrestling with the consequences of escaped vigor. Some plants know no bounds. A plant advertised as "rapidly spreading" might also be considered invasive, which is the horticultural equivalent of squirrels at the bird feeder. Most invasive plants rapidly spread by means of underground stems and/or roots and are not readily stopped.

Bittersweeet, gooseneck loosestrife *(Lysimachia),* mint, and bee balm are examples of plants often considered invasive. The same holds true for purple loosestrife (*Lythrum* species) and bamboo. These plants will always try to take more room than you (or your neighbors) want to give them.

Some vigorous plants can be restrained by pruning vigilantly or by installing an impenetrable barrier, such as sheet metal, 16 inches deep in the planting bed. The important aspect of managing any invasive plant is knowing its characteristics before you plant it.

SPECIAL REQUIREMENTS

It is impossible to know what questions to ask about every plant. Sometimes it's helpful to ask, "Have you grown this plant before and does it need any special care?"

An open-ended question like this may turn up solid information, especially if the other party has personal experience with the plant.

If you have moved to a different part of the country, be sure to talk about your gardening plans. Ask your neighbors lots of questions. Long-time gardeners are quick to share hands-on horticultural lore and are likely to steer you away from locally troublesome plants. Favorite plants from your previous home may not fare as well in the new neighborhood as you do.

INSECT AND DISEASE SUSCEPTIBILITY

Diseases and infestations tend to be opportunistic. They most often arise from weakness in the plant created by physical injury or by cultural circumstances such as poor drainage. Some species are more prone to insects and diseases than others. The vulnerability of plants may increase or decrease with your geographic location.

Before purchasing a plant, try to discover if it has any notable problems when grown in your area. Ask garden center personnel directly if the plant is especially susceptible to any insects or diseases. While you should always expect some gnawing and nibbling in the garden, you want to avoid plants that are magnets for trouble.

Once you know, you may decide that it's worth playing plant doctor for some species. The handsome evergreen shrub Japanese andromeda *(Pieris japonica)* is nearly carefree in the middle and lower South, but lacewing infestations cause havoc in the mid-Atlantic and the East. You'll have to decide whether you love the plant enough to take on the extra care it will need.

Chapter 7

A Primer on Planting

Good dirt and correct planting make gardening easier and more rewarding over time. Better soil makes better plants, helping them develop strong root systems for healthier, faster growth and better drought tolerance. Here's how to get your plants off to a fine start.

Sampling Soil

Submitting soil samples for scientific testing is the only way to find out exactly what additions your soil needs to be a good growing medium. Soil tests determine the acidity (pH) of the soil, the proportion of organic matter, and the amounts of nitrogen, phosphate, potassium, and other elements. Typical test readouts provide a recipe for supplemental nutrients.

Soil testing is available through your county's Agricultural Extension Service office and sometimes at garden centers. Allow several weeks for test results to be returned.

Smaller self-test kits are available from garden centers. Though not as precise, these kits provide informative results immediately.

This small garden shows how rich in plant texture, form, and color a little space can be.

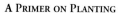

DIGGING IN

Good garden soil is easily worked, well drained, rich in nutrients, and able to retain some moisture. It has a texture like pie-crust dough before the water is added. If the soil has all of these attributes and is 12 inches deep, the garden is in very good shape. (The soil in the container of a purchased perennial will give you an idea of the texture of an effective growing mix.)

You will probably need to amend and work the soil to make it suitable for long-term gardening. If you can prepare all the soil early on, the heavy work will be out of the way once and for all. Plan to do soil prep before you buy plants and allow at least a weekend for the job.

MAKING GOOD EARTH

Soil is easiest to work if it is slightly moist and if all vegetation has been removed. Grass is most easily removed by spraying with a nonselective herbicide ten days before you plan to dig. (These herbicides decompose into harmless compounds once they reach the ground.) After the vegetation dies, it is easily removed for disposal.

Dig up unwanted plants and sod and remove them, roots and all. Turn the soil in the planting area as deeply as possible with a shovel, a gardener's mattock, or a tiller. Turning it at least 12 inches deep is best.

Heavy clay soils (earth that clings to the shovel in clumps) need to have a lot of organic matter added to break up the glutinous texture and allow plant roots to spread easily and breathe. These soils require the most work to prepare.

The technique is simple. After turning the bed, spread a 3-inch layer of well-rotted sawdust, leaf mold, or compost over it. (In the South, finely pulverized pine bark, frequently sold under the label "soil

Take the time and make the effort to prepare your garden soil thoroughly. Dig 12 inches deep and turn the soil over.

First Things First

If you don't know where your utility lines are buried, call your utility locator service before you dig. This service temporarily marks the *approximate* location of any underground lines, which is the best way to avoid severing one.

Don't assume that the markings are exact. Proceed cautiously when digging within one foot of a marking.

Also, never rely on the line being buried to the correct depth. Simply because a utility line *should* be 18 inches beneath the surface doesn't mean that it actually is.

If you must dig near a line, use a hand trowel to visually expose it. Once you see it, you can avoid hitting it with heavier tools.

conditioner" is an economical, easily assimilated material.) Till or work this material in thoroughly and repeat the process until the soil does not aggregate in pieces much larger than a marble. You are trying to create a growing medium that has a mealy texture.

Poor, sandy soils also require organic matter to retain moisture and nutrients. Amending these soils is usually much easier than dealing with clay soils. Use organic compost, manure, or peat moss as additives. Peat moss is terrific for water retention; manure is superb for enrichment. Compost does both jobs.

As you add organic matter to sandy soils, the mix will show some tendency to clump after moistening, though not nearly as much as "lightened" clay soils.

After you have finished preparing the soil, rake the beds smooth and relax — you've earned it.

Use a small tiller to mix in all the soil amendments your soil needs. This one-time effort will pay off handsomely later.

WHAT TO LOOK FOR IN PLANTS

After the beds are prepared, it's time to go shopping for plants. Here's a primer on selecting them and a bit about planting them.

Trees, shrubs, and herbaceous perennials are sold as balled-and-burlapped plants, container-grown stock, or bare-root plants. Balled-and-burlapped plants have been dug from a growing field. The ball of earth surrounding the roots is wrapped with burlap cloth to keep it from cracking, crumbling, or otherwise shattering the root structure of the plant. Most large plants are sold this way.

The best time to buy these plants is in midspring, shortly after the foliage has started to show on deciduous plants. Buy only plants that show leaves on all the branches. Under these conditions you know that the plant is alive and that the root system, cut when the plant was dug in the field, is in good shape, too.

Carry balled-and-burlapped plants by supporting the root ball. If the plant is too heavy to lift, have the nursery deliver it — after you dig the hole. Keep in mind that heavy plants are awkward to plant. Consider hiring the nursery to dig, plant, mulch, and guarantee large balled-and-burlapped plants, especially if they are important to the garden scheme.

Picking Healthy Plants

Looks are everything in selecting a plant: a healthy plant *looks* healthy. The foliage should be uniform in color; the plant should look robust and perky, with no withering or drooping leaves. Twigs should be supple, and there should be no broken or crushed branches. The visible soil in the container should be firm and moist, never dry, cracked, crumbling, or weed filled. Avoid plants that have a lot of roots growing out the drain holes at the bottom of the container.

If you are shopping for a balled-and-burlapped plant, the ball should be covered with sawdust or mulched and the covering should be moist. The burlap should wrap the soil snugly. There should be no large roots protruding from the side of the burlap, and the earth ball should be firm and solid. Avoid a plant that has a loose, dried, or crumbling earth ball. Feeder roots projecting through the burlap are a good indication of the plant's vigor.

Most nursery plants are grown in black plastic pots, between 1 and 10 gallons in size. These plants have a healthy balance between the contained root system and the visible crown. They are usually vigorous and ready to transplant into the garden. There is no seasonal restriction on planting container plants, but it is important to choose a time when you will be around to water them.

As for size, pick a container that you can easily load and handle. Smaller plants, which are usually younger, will be more vigorous and resilient than larger ones. Unless you need a large plant immediately, select smaller ones. They are reliable, less expensive, and easier to handle.

Perennials and specialty plants from mail-order outlets are often sold as bare-root plants. Instead of soil, moistened sawdust or wood shavings cover the roots. Garden centers may carry a few bare-root plants on a seasonal basis. Before purchasing one, check the roots to be sure they are not dry. You can't dawdle with bare-root plants. Soak the roots while digging the planting site and plant immediately.

Ground covers and bedding plants are usually sold in small, segmented plastic trays, known as cell packs, that hold eight to twelve individual plants. Each plant is individually rooted and must be kept moist. When you are ready to plant, you simply pop out the "cube" of roots and soil.

PLANTING

You've already done the hard work, preparing the planting bed to a depth of 12 inches — ahem — well, if you stopped at 8 inches, that will do. After this, planting is easy.

Dig a hole at least twice as large as the root ball or the diameter of the container. The wider the better; you want the plant's roots to spread out and feed in the top 8 to 10 inches of soil.

Do not dig deeper than the root ball is tall because you do not want the plant to settle lower than the surface of the bed and so become a low spot where rainwater collects. Slice into the sides of the hole with a shovel to loosen the earth and encourage root expansion.

Place balled-and-burlapped plants so that the top of the root ball is at least 1½ inches above the top of the hole. Turn the plant so that it faces the way you want it to. Remove any twine or cord binding the trunk or branches and loosen the burlap from the top of the plant. Fold the burlap back from the top of the plant far enough so that it does not protrude above the ground after you fill the hole.

Never remove the burlap, since this keeps the root ball intact. While natural-fiber burlap will decompose, synthetic burlap will restrict root growth. Cut synthetic burlap vertically several times around the root ball before you plant. The last step is to refill the hole with soil, mounding it over the exposed sides of the root ball.

The procedure for container-grown plants is exactly the same as above. First, however, you must gently remove the container from the plant by holding both upside down and letting the plant slide easily out of the container. Cut off any roots that have grown through the drainage holes of the container.

Sometimes older container-grown plants have thick matted roots that have pressed against the side of the container. Break up that matted root mass by pulling them free, especially in the bottom third of the container. You may have to be forceful; in fact, you should cut any roots growing in a circular direction

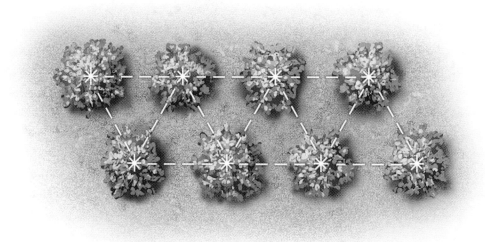

Spacing plants equidistantly in staggered rows will allow them to grow together and fill the bed evenly.

around the ball or "unwind" them and direct them away from the root ball into the sides of the hole.

Cell-pack plants frequently have matted roots, which can easily be loosened by hand. Use a trowel to loosen the bed to the proper depth, then position the plant so that the top is level with the surface. Firm the soil around the top of the plant with your fingers.

MULCHING

Mulching reduces moisture loss through evaporation, lessens the extremes of summer and winter temperatures, helps keep the soil workable, and reduces weedy growth. A good organic mulch will also decompose to enrich the soil. Mulch is horticulturally good stuff. In a small garden it also serves as a unifying and decorative element.

A mulch with a dark, uniform color makes an excellent backdrop for flowers. I have found that a finely textured material, such as pulverized pine bark, which is a more finely processed product than typical ground bark mulch, or

Setting plants, especially shrubs, in the ground slightly above grade guards against poor drainage and encourages wide-spreading root systems.

Mulch

Prepared soil

Native soil

Keeping Plants Healthy

Over the life of a garden, the best defense against insects and disease is healthy plants, properly planted and well attended. Even these steps can't protect all plants from infestation. You may be able to minimize problems by avoiding older cultivars that are disease-prone and seeking newer varieties that promise or demonstrate disease resistance.

If a plant develops signs of disease or insect problems, have it properly diagnosed by taking samples of the infested or damaged part (placed in a Ziploc bag) to a local garden center or county extension center. (Or you may be able to consult reference volumes with photographs or drawings of common disease and pest damage.)

Once the problem is properly diagnosed, treat it first with the mildest product available, such as an insecticidal soap or something similar. (See *Taylor's Weekend Guide to Organic Pest and Disease Control.*) Regardless of the treatment method you choose, always read the product label before purchasing a product to make sure it is correct for your problem and safe enough to have around the house. Always follow the manufacturer's recommendations on usage. You may have to contact your local Agricultural Extension Service for particularly troublesome insect or disease problems.

well-rotted sawdust (which will be black in color), makes an excellent mulch. You can apply these materials easily and evenly to bedding plants and viny ground covers by pouring them between plants.

You should apply 2 to 3 inches of mulch. In areas where you expect to plant bulbs or bedding plants, choose a fine-textured mulch that is easy to work with a trowel or your fingers. Harder-to-work-mulches, such as pine straw or coarse bark, are better used in areas where you don't plan to cultivate frequently. Commercially packaged mulches are sold in 3-cubic-foot bags that are easily transported in a passenger car.

Never pile mulch directly against the trunks of trees or the bases of plants. Pull it back a few inches.

Essential Water

Water new plants thoroughly after planting, using a steady flow directed to the base of the stems until the planting hole is saturated. This is the only method that delivers water down into the roots. You should water new plantings this way for a full calendar year. Use a shower-head nozzle or a fine-spray flow adapter to provide a high volume of water in a steady flow, like that from a traditional watering can.

Once plants are established (typically one full growing season) and the root system has spread into the soil surrounding the root ball, you may switch to watering with a lawn sprinkler.

Soaker hoses, which exude water slowly throughout their length, can work well for small gardens. Weave them through the plantings and cover them with mulch.

CHAPTER 8

PLANTS FOR SPECIAL USES

Based on their size at maturity, there are hundreds of plants that are ideal for small gardens. The challenge is to narrow the list of possible plants to those that will fill your specific requirements. Not only do you want the chosen plants to work well, but you want them to bring a suitable level of excitement to the garden.

Suggestions for solving common planting problems are offered below. The listed plants are proven, rewarding ornamentals suitable for a wide range of geographical conditions. The plants listed here that correspond to your hardiness zone may not be the most widely known ornamentals at your local garden center, but they will probably make the local nursery's short list.

TREES FOR SMALL GARDENS

If there is room in your garden for a tree, you would probably like to have one that will provide both shade and beauty and that will thrive in a small space. If you have room for just one tree, the choice may be really difficult.

Shade is probably the most important contribution a tree can make. Shade reduces heat buildup by filtering sunlight and may reduce glare and reflection

This Charleston garden has a formal plan yet a relaxed demeanor. It's a garden that wants to chat rather than give a lecture.

from walking surfaces. In the mid-Atlantic, South, and Southwest, shade is a necessity. Remember, it's not essential to block out the sun completely; you just want to interrupt the hottest, most direct rays coming into the garden.

You should plant the tree so that its foliage will grow between your garden and the sun. The optimum placement is usually on the south or southwest side of the garden (or of a sitting area).

Avoid any tree likely to grow taller than 30 feet. It may provide great shade quickly, but the root systems are likely to cause problems as they mature.

The list of suitable trees for a small garden varies across the country. Here is a checklist of qualities that you might want to look for in a small-space tree.

- Tolerance for direct sun and high heat
- Reliable hardiness for a long life in your region
- Fine-textured foliage, which will provide light shade
- High branching, forming an upright spreading or umbrella-shaped canopy
- Ornamental qualities such as flowers, handsome branch structure, or ornamental bark
- Either fruit enjoyed by birds or no dropping fruit or twigs

City planning departments frequently have lists of trees approved for local street plantings. As in a small garden, street trees must thrive in restricted root space, be modest in size, be resistant to disease and drought, and not prone to dropping twigs or fruit.

Five Trees to Shade Small Gardens

The following trees grow at a moderate rate, have branch structures and crown shapes favorable for patio use, and are dependable over a wide geographical area. Your local garden center can broaden this list with other species for your immediate region.

- *Acer tataricum* ssp. *ginnala* / Amur maple
  Zone 3
  Amur maple has a wide crown with glossy green foliage that turns vivid red in fall. The flowers have a sweet fragrance, unusual for maples. The winged fruits turn red in late summer while the foliage is still green.

Shade Without Trees

Some gardens lack sufficient space for a tree's roots or have little overhead room for the branches. If you cannot plant a tree, consider creating shade by building an arbor or overhead lattice. These timeless architectural solutions to the problem of providing shade can serve a small garden permanently without taking up precious room needed for walking. When covered with vines, these structures make a green roof over all or a portion of the garden.

An arbor is a free-standing structure with a trellis support for climbing vines. It can be as simple as two posts connected at the top by a pair of ornamental beams high enough to walk under. Crosspieces on the top of the beams and sometimes on the posts serve as the trellis support for climbing vines. An arbor can shade a gate or entryway or can be positioned at the end of a garden view.

An overhead lattice is a variation on the arbor concept that shades a larger area. Basically it is a wooden frame for climbing plants. The lattice may be supported by four posts or may be attached to the house on one side with posts on the opposite side.

Arbors and overhead lattice structures may be very simple or ornate, custom built or pre-fabricated. There are many designs suitable for any garden style. One key requirement is any support posts be made from preservative-treated wood that is suitable for use in the ground.

- *Cercis canadensis* / Redbud
  Zone 5

  Redbud is a tough native with a naturally umbrella-shaped crown. Pea-shaped magenta flowers bloom along the branches in early to midspring. The heart-shaped leaves turn yellow in fall.

- *Koelreuteria paniculata* / Golden-rain tree
  Zone 5

  Golden-rain tree offers sprays of bright yellow flowers in the dead heat of summer and deep shade beneath its umbrella form. The fruits, which look like Japanese lanterns, remain through fall.

■ *Pistacia chinensis* / Chinese pistache

Zone 7, perhaps 6

Chinese pistache throws a light shade from an umbrella-shaped canopy. The largest of this group of small-space trees, it has small leaves that turn vivid orange to red in fall. Dependable in hot, dry settings.

■ *Prunus serrulata* × *kwanzan* / Kwanzan cherry

Zone 6

Kwanzan cherry is widely used for commercial plantings, testimony to its reliability. The tree is celebrated for its double pink flowers, handsome bark, upright growth habit, and orange-red fall color with no mess and no fuss.

PLANTS AS SCULPTURE OR ACCENTS

Plants with bold, eye-catching forms can be used as living sculpture in the garden. While this is obvious where evergreen plants are concerned, it can be a pleasant bonus from deciduous trees and shrubs.

Plan to use the subtle beauty of a plant's branching architecture, bark coloration, and fruit. A tree or shrub with sculptural branches can turn a nondescript corner into a feature of calligraphy.

I find that multitrunk trees or trees that branch low to the ground have a greater ornamental value than trees that branch high from a single trunk. The following trees have armature that is exceptionally attractive.

■ *Acer palmatum* / Japanese maple

Zone 5

This tree deserves to be in the center of the garden. The muscular branching and lovely foliage of the species provide a refined beauty. The brilliant red fall foliage color is unsurpassed. Many cultivars are available to suit any garden size.

■ *Lagerstroemia indica* / Crape myrtle

Zone 7

Crape myrtle brings a spectacular show of colorful bloom to hot, dry locations. Rapid growers, these trees possess exquisite branching and bark when mature. New hybrids such as 'Natchez' are top of the line. Buy crape myrtles in summer, when they are in bloom, to be sure of the color.

Turn a Shrub into a Tree

Gardening is full of cheap thrills, and pruning a big, cheap evergreen shrub into an artful tree form is one of them.

Evergreen shrubs that exceed 10 feet in height and width, not uncommon from Zone 7 south, are too large for a small garden. By pruning the lower branches, you can create a handsome, multitrunked evergreen tree with an exquisite branch structure. In less than an hour you can transform a plant you want to kill to a plant others would die for.

In a new garden, plant large-maturing, fast-growing shrubs with the intention of pruning them into trees. You get sculptural bark as well as the constancy of evergreens — very often more quickly and at lower cost than a tree. Here are a few evergreens to consider, but any that will grow large quickly where you live will do.

- *Ilex cornuta* 'Burfordii' / Burford holly
  15 feet
  Zone 7.
- *Ligustrum japonicum* / Japanese privet
  12–15 feet
  Zone 7
- *Myrica cerifera* / Southern wax myrtle
  10–15 feet
  Zone 7

California gardeners can use California wax myrtle *(M. californicus),* a native species that is similar.

Presto chango — a shrub becomes a tree. By pruning off the lower branches, you reveal the larger trunks and create a living sculpture.

■ *Magnolia* × *soulangeana* / Saucer magnolia
Zone 6
This deciduous magnolia, heralded for its large spring flowers, does not receive enough kudos for its sculptural form, especially in the northern end of its range.

■ *Viburnum plicatum* var. *tomentosum* / Doublefile viburnum
Zone 5
Midway between a tree and a shrub in size, doublefile viburnum grows rapidly to 8 or 10 feet tall and slightly wider. It is multitrunked and has horizontal branching. Flowers are carried in rows above deep green foliage on the top of each branch.

The art of topiary has pushed the boundaries of living sculpture to ever more fanciful forms. Use topiaries sparingly and carefully because they can skew the tone of the garden. The joy of a topiary is surprise. Too many of them diminishes the impact. Spiral-pruned junipers and "poodled" junipers are just such garden punctuation marks.

Some evergreen trees with unusual form need a background to temper their radical chic. Weeping blue Atlas cedar (*Cedrus atlantica* 'Glauca pendula'), Hollywood juniper (*Juniperus chinensis* 'Torulosa'), and Grey's weeping yaupon (*Ilex vomitoria* 'Pendula') are so unusual-looking that the garden is best served if they are planted in front of a backdrop.

LOOKING FOR COVER

Ground covers serve as the carpet in the garden room, unifying the composition with their texture, color, and flowers. Ground covers are distinguished from other plants by what they do, not what they are. The plants can be expected to spread and cover a whole planting area.

As a design element, ground covers are easy to use. A simple, satisfying combination is a small tree, a few shrubs, and several perennials in an established ground cover planting. It's an easy look to create and maintain, and it rarely is tiring to the eyes.

Ground covers are usually not fussy about growing conditions. Match the plant to the amount of sun in the garden. Till or turn the soil thoroughly to

encourage rapid growth, set the plants at the recommended spacing, then apply a good cover of mulch. Once established, ground covers require little maintenance and may restrict weed growth.

There are oodles of possible choices among the woody shrubs, vines, and herbaceous perennials, both evergreen and deciduous. Garden centers always have an array of ground covers for all horticultural conditions. It can be hard to choose among them. The ground covers below do not exceed 12 inches in height and can be expected to create a dense mat of foliage.

Some Deciduous Ground Covers

- *Convallaria majalis* / Lily-of-the-valley
  Zone 2
  Refer to the listing under fragrant perennials, page 109. Part sun or shade.

- *Galium oderatum* / Sweet woodruff
  Zones 2–3
  A dressy, dainty carpet of foliage — whorled dark green leaves on upright stems reaching to 9 inches tall. White flowers emerge at the top in spring. Sweet woodruff spreads quickly by underground runners and does well in part sun or shade in any soil.

- *Hosta* species / Hosta
  Zone 4
  Hostas emerge as a clump of leaves from an ever-enlarging center. Varietal differences offer foliage heights between 6 inches and 3 feet and a variety of leaf shapes, textures, and colors. Tube-shaped flowers, either white or lavender (some are fragrant), appear on tall stalks in summer. Planted close together, hostas create a solid-looking ground cover. They need full shade to part sun in well-drained loose soil.

- *Lamium maculatum* / Lamium; Dead nettle
  Zone 4
  This diminutive spreading perennial with heart-shaped toothed leaves is an old reliable — and tough. Growing to 12 inches tall, it spreads quickly but not relentlessly. The tube-shaped flowers bloom intermittently from spring through summer. Plant in sun or shade in moist soil. It will also survive in dry sites.

Some Evergreen Ground Covers

- *Ajuga reptans* / Bugleweed
  Zone 3
  Bugleweed forms a low mat of foliage that spreads vigorously across the ground. Spikes of purple, white, or blue flowers top the plants in early summer. Plant in full sun or shade in ordinary soil.

- *Juniperus horizontalis* 'Wiltonii' / Blue rug juniper
  Zone 2
  This dressy, hard-nosed juniper can take extreme cold. It grows moderately quickly to create a silvery blue mat. Many junipers are suitable for use as ground covers. Plant them in well-drained soil in full or part sun.

- *Liriope spicata* / Creeping lilyturf
  Zone 6 or 5
  Lilyturf quickly spreads to form a grassy mat of ¼-inch-wide leaves up to 18 inches long. It is a vigorous plant that looks sleek and grows well in any well-drained soil.

- *Pachysandra terminalis* / Japanese spurge
  Zone 4
  Japanese spurge has dressy, deep green leaves that are thick and fleshy. It spreads rapidly by underground stems to form an impenetrable mat 8 inches tall. Plant in part sun or shade in ordinary soil. Mulching with pulverized materials seems to encourage the plant to spread.

- *Trachelospermum asiaticum* / Asian jasmine
  Zone 8
  This delicate-looking plant has a Texas-sized tolerance for sun and heat. The foliage is small and glossy on tough, wiry stems. Asian jasmine grows into a low, dense mat of foliage that retains a neat look all year. Plant in sun or shade.

- *Vinca minor* / Periwinkle
  Zone 4
  Periwinkle is a handsome viny plant that grows into a cheery-looking tangle that is quite dressy. In formal or informal settings it provides great reward for

the effort. Lavender flowers appear in spring. Plant in any soil, with any sun exposure, though partial sun to shade is best in the South.

PLANTS FOR ARCHITECTURE

The tangled, seemingly boundless energy of vines epitomizes garden exuberance. Because it is their nature to drape or cling, vines blur the hard edges of architecture, draping both romance and a sense of timelessness about the garden. Vines smooth the transition from the built world to the soft earth.

A particular virtue of vines is their vertical vigor; they provide a fast, inexpensive way to bring foliage, flower, and fruit to high places. They can be used as a living wallpaper or ceiling and some are commendable ground covers.

Vines can provide shade if you lack room for a tree: build an arbor or support structure and plant vines to cover. They can cool a garden: plant them on a wall to reduce glare and reflect heat, keeping the wall and the earth at its base cooler. Good vines not only make good walls, they can mask average carpentry — or an unsightly mailbox.

Vines climb in different ways. Some have modified roots that adhere to surfaces; some twine tendrils around supports, such as wire or fishing line; others wrap their stems around an object and twist into the sky. You must know how a vine climbs to provide the proper support.

Some vines are too vigorous for small gardens. Bittersweet and wisteria are industrial-strength. They need heavy support structures and may escape and become a nuisance.

Vines That Climb by Tendrils or Twining

Many durable vines are in this category, including wild grape, Hall's honeysuckle, and native wisteria, three vines that are too rampant to manage easily. The following vines are widely distributed and reliable. Their popularity is well deserved.

- *Clematis* hybrids / Hybrid clematis
  Zone 5
  Well known in the South as the "mailbox plant," the numerous hybrids boast extraordinary floral variety, with blossoms from 3 to 8 inches wide in white, pink, red, purple, and blue. Plant clematis in full sun in a location where the roots

are shaded. They prefer well-drained, moist soil. The leaf petioles of clematis serve the same function as tendrils.

- *Gelsemium sempervirens* / Carolina yellow jessamine
  Zone 7–8
  This durable, fast-climbing evergreen produces profuse, fragrant yellow flowers in spring. Glossy narrow leaves turn purple in winter. Plant in ordinary soil in full or part sun.

- *Lonicera × heckrottii* / Goldflame honeysuckle
  Zone 5
  This semi-evergreen honeysuckle produces clusters of slender, tube-shaped, fragrant flowers from late spring through summer. The blossoms are red outside, yellow inside. Plant in full or part sun in any well-drained soil.

- *Polygonum aubertii* / Silver fleece vine
  Zone 5
  This airy deciduous vine is covered with clusters of small fragrant flowers in midsummer. It grows and covers rapidly but will freeze back to the ground in the North. Plant in full or part sun in any well-drained soil.

Vines That Cling or Adhere

The modified roots by which vines adhere can eventually degrade wood siding and masonry, but they take a long time to cause significant damage. I suppose it is better to plant these vines where damage is not an issue, such as a concrete-block wall or a fence. Still, don't be dissuaded from growing them where you want them. In a small garden, how much damage can they do?

Every three years or so you should cut these vines back to the ground and let them ascend again. This keeps the look fresh and offers a chance to examine the structure the vines are growing on.

- *Ficus pumila* / Climbing fig
  Zone 8
  This is the delicate evergreen vine of coastal southern courtyards. It forms an exquisite soft "wallpaper" on brick or stucco, with the heart-shaped leaves overlapping like green scales. Plant in moist, well-drained soil and shelter from hot afternoon sun.

- *Hedera helix* / English ivy

  Zone 6 or 5

  This resilient, vigorous vine, with various leaf shapes and colors, is sturdy, elegant, and a fabulous climber. Some cultivars are excellent as ground covers. Plant in sun (in the North only) or shade (even deep shade) in ordinary soil. Ivy spreads rapidly once it is established.

- *Hydrangea anomala* ssp. *petiolaris* / Climbing hydrangea

  Zone 5

  This woody, sculptural deciduous vine rewards patience. It produces clusters of white flowers 6 to 8 inches wide in summer. The round leaves are a deep, glossy green. It is very tolerant of different sun exposures, but needs moist, rich, well-drained soil. It grows slowly, so don't prune it; it's worth the wait.

- *Parthenocissus tricuspidata* / Boston ivy

  Zone 2

  This is an easy vine that clings vigorously to any surface. The glossy green maple-leaf-shaped leaves absolutely ignite in scarlet in autumn before falling. Plant in part sun or shade in ordinary soil.

Chapter 9

Distinctive Shrubs, Fragrant Plants, and Favored Perennials

Shrubs Adaptable to Small Gardens

Shrubs should be easy to grow and manage but not boring. Since space is precious, look for plants that bring more to the garden tableau than a single season's interest.

There are many, many fine shrubs in every region and hardiness zone. I offer a few excellent plants, distinguished for being attractive in several seasons and relatively trouble-free to grow. They are further commended because they adapt to many different design schemes. If left untouched, a few of them (or certain cultivars derived from the species) will push the size limits of small garden spaces. Some deft pruning will keep them in bounds easily.

Showy sedum, an elegant, tough perennial, headlines this festive border. It teams with marigold and monarch daisies, another top-of-the-line perennial for small spaces.

Deciduous Shrubs

■ *Berberis thunbergii* 'Atropurpurea Nana' / Crimson pygmy barberry
  Full sun
  Zone 4

This barberry grows at a moderate rate to a compact rounded shape, 2 to 3 feet high and slightly wider. The burgundy foliage is fine-textured; the twigs are spiny. The plant blends well with shrubs or perennials. It is reliable in hot, dry locations. Plant in average, well-drained soil. 'Kobold', with rich green foliage, and 'Aurea', with bright gold leaves, are also excellent small-space barberries.

■ *Hydrangea quercifolia* / Oakleaf hydrangea
  Part sun to shade
  Zone 5

An adaptable native southeastern shrub, oakleaf hydrangea grows slowly into an upright irregular form 6 to 8 feet tall and wide. The coarse-textured oaklike leaves turn rich, deep shades of red in autumn. Large panicles of white midsummer flowers turn blush rose in autumn. The stems have peeling, parchment-colored bark. Though large, this shrub is always a winner. It prefers rich, loamy soil high in organic matter. 'Snow Queen' is a denser, smaller cultivar that is excellent for small settings.

■ *Itea virginica* / Virginia sweetspire
  Full to part sun
  Zone 5

Virginia sweetspire grows into an irregular upright form 3 to 5 feet high and slightly less wide. The plant bears upright clusters of fragrant flowers on reddish twigs in midsummer. The deep green foliage turns vivid scarlet in fall. Plant in good garden soil with plenty of organic matter. It prefers moist conditions and is very durable.

■ *Spirea japonica* / Japanese spirea
  Full or part sun
  Zone 3

These delicate-looking dwarf shrubs are noted for their dainty summer flowers, attractive small leaves, and toughness. The plants grow 2 to 3 feet tall and wide and appear as a fine-textured mound. Tiny flowers at the tops of twigs range in color from white to deep pink. Plant in average, well-drained garden soil. There are many cultivars, including 'Anthony Waterer', with deep pink flowers and green foliage, and 'Goldflame', with bright yellow foliage and rose flowers. Look also for 'Little Princess' and 'Nana', dwarf cultivars with pink flowers.

Evergreen Shrubs

- *Leucothoe axillaris* / Coastal leucothoe
  Part sun or shade
  Zone 4
  This handsome shrub, with spreading arching stems and leathery, glossy leaves, mounds 2 to 4 feet high and slightly wider. The foliage turns maroon in colder weather. Delicate bell-shaped flowers in 1- to 2-inch clusters rise from the base of the leaf stalks in late spring. Plant in moist, well-drained soil rich in organic matter, and shelter from hot summer sun. Drooping leucothoe *(L. fontanesiana)*, a southeastern mountain native, is manageable for small gardens but needs a cooler site.

- *Mahonia bealei* / Leatherleaf mahonia
  Part shade
  Zone 6
  Leatherleaf mahonia grows slowly to 8 feet or more as a group of woody canes topped with whorls of lengthy compound leaves, each leaf with 9 to 12 glossy, blue-green spiny leaflets. Bright yellow flowers top the canes in early spring, followed by bright blue fruit. In too small a space, it can seem over-bearing. Oregon grape holly *(M. aquifolium)* is smaller and just as good-looking but less architectural. Plant both in average, well-drained soil sheltered from direct summer sun and winter winds. Remove tall canes to keep mahonia from getting overgrown.

- *Nandina domestica* / Heavenly bamboo; Nandina
  Full to part sun
  Zone 7
  Nandina grows into a clump of stiff upright twigs 5 to 6 feet tall, topped with delicate dressy foliage. The compound leaves vary in color from reddish

bronze to deep green and crimson or purple through the year. Profuse small white flowers become sprays of red berries. Nandina prefers average to rich soil and regular water. Many dwarf forms are suitable in the front of a border: 'Harbor Dwarf' stays under 2 feet tall; 'Nana' grows slightly taller. 'Atropurpurea Nana' has brightly colored foliage in cool weather.

- *Pieris japonica* / Japanese andromeda
  Part sun to shade
  Zone 6

This dressy shrub grows slowly to more than 9 feet tall and 6 feet wide. Whorls of deep green foliage are covered with long clusters of small white-to-pink flowers in early spring. The season's new leaves open with a red flush, gradually changing to dark green. Andromeda's only disadvantage is its susceptibility to lace bugs, which are easily controlled. Plant in well-drained soil rich in organic matter, sheltered from direct sun. Smaller cultivars include 'Bisbee Dwarf', 'Dorothy Wycoff', 'John's Select', and 'Pygmaea'. Look also for 'Brouwer's Beauty', a low-growing hybrid with more horizontal flower clusters.

- *Raphiolepis indica* / Indian hawthorn
  Full to part sun
  Zone 8

This prim-looking but tough plant grows slowly to a mound about 4 feet tall and wide. Indian hawthorn loves heat and withstands salt spray after it is established. The leaves are glossy dark green with slightly toothed margins. The soft pink, slightly fragrant flowers appear in late spring and mature to blue berries. Plant in average soil that will drain. 'Enchantress' is a compact cultivar with pink flowers.

- *Rhododendron* species and hybrids / Rhododendron
  Part shade
  Zone 5

Rhododendrons bring stately foliage and prolific bloom to the garden. They grow at a moderate rate into an upright, rounded form 3 to 8 feet tall and wide. Some grow much larger. While the showy blooms in late spring or early summer might seem to be everything, it is the handsome, glossy leaves, 4 to 6 inches long, that best commend these plants. The flowers form clusters known as trusses on top of whorls of foliage. Flower color ranges from white to yellow, pink, red, lavender, and purple. Rhododendrons thrive in moist, well-drained, slightly acidic soil rich in organic matter. Avoid exposures with direct, hot summer sun. Look for these smaller (under 4 feet) cultivars. Red flowers: 'Elizabeth' and 'Scarlet Wonder'; pink: 'Bow Bells', 'Olga Mezitt', and 'Waltham'; lavender: 'Blue Diamond', 'PJM', and 'Ramapo'; white: 'Anna H. Hall', 'Chionoides', and 'Dora Amateis'.

PLANTS WITH OUTSTANDING FRAGRANCE

If you have to choose between a fragrant and a nonfragrant plant, let your nose cast the deciding vote. Fragrance broadens our sensory experience and brings another dimension to enjoyment of the garden. The invisible charms of fragrance slip through the back door of our consciousness. If a scent reminds you of a favorite place, as is often the case, the garden appeals not only to the here and now, but to fond yesterdays as well.

The greatest selection of fragrant plants is found among the shrubs, vines, and perennials. Select at least one or two fragrant plants per season; it's nice to move through the garden calendar with a parade of different scents. A little overlap in bloom is rarely a problem. Flower fragrances are rarely so powerful that the effect is cloying or nose-tickling. Leave room to plant some fragrant annuals, which can also add to the garden's perfume.

The only disclaimer here is that fragrance, whether in an elevator or in a garden, is a matter of personal preference. Perhaps you should sniff before you decide to buy.

Fragrant Deciduous Shrubs

■ *Clethra alnifolia* / Sweet pepperbush
 Summer
 Zone 5
 This tough deciduous shrub is upright and stemmy in form, growing slowly to as much as 9 feet tall. In midsummer, upright 4- to 6-inch-long clusters of tiny, extremely sweet-smelling white flowers appear. There are cultivars with pink and rose flowers. Plant in full or part sun in average soil. Clethra prefers moist conditions and will tolerate a wet site.

■ *Rhododendron viscosum* / Swamp azalea
Early summer
Zone 6
This native deciduous azalea grows at a moderate rate to 6 feet tall, forming an open, twiggy crown about 4 feet wide. The white flowers, appearing in clusters at the tips of branches in early to midsummer, have a lovely perfume. The plant is very statuesque and looks best planted in a ground-cover bed or silhouetted against a fence or wall. Plant in a moist soil rich in organic matter in partial sun. The fragrant Atlantic azalea *(R. atlanticum)* grows to 3 feet, has blue-green foliage, and is hardy to Zone 5.

■ *Syringa laciniata* / Cut-leaf lilac
Spring
Zone 4
This lilac, named for the deeply cut leaves, brings a light dose of a favorite fragrance in a shrub of manageable size for small gardens. It grows moderately fast to about 4 to 6 feet tall and wide. Clusters of pink to rose flowers bloom along the branches in early spring. Plant in full or part sun in ordinary soil.

■ *Viburnum carlesii* / Korean spice viburnum
Spring
Zone 4
   This sturdy shrub grows at a moderate rate to 4 or 5 feet tall and wide. The wonderfully fragrant white flowers emerge from pink buds to form dome-shaped clusters as the leaves emerge in early spring. Dwarf selections are available. Judd viburnum *(V. × juddii)* is very similar but grows larger. Both viburnums grow best in full or part sun, preferring well-drained soil.

Fragrant Evergreen Shrubs

■ *Daphne odora* / Winter daphne
Late winter
Zone 7
A very dapper evergreen with the most intoxicating fragrance, winter daphne grows slowly into a globe 4 feet tall and wide covered with 3-inch-long glossy

leaves. Flower buds are clustered at the ends of twigs and open deep rose or white in early winter. The related garland flower *(D. cneorum)* grows into a low mat less than 1 foot tall and 2 to 4 feet wide. Hardy to Zone 4, it blooms in spring, showing clusters of fragrant, star-shaped pink flowers. Where summers are very hot, these plants grow better in part sun. Though these daphnes are not fussy about soil, good drainage is an absolute must.

■ *Gardenia jasminoides* 'Radicans' / Dwarf or trailing gardenia
Summer
Zone 8
This gloriously fragrant gardenia grows slowly to 2 or 3 feet high and about 4 feet wide. With small, fine-textured, glossy leaves, it is a beautiful small shrub. The 2-inch, waxy white flowers bloom continuously for an extended period in summer. Plant in partial to full sun in fertile, well-drained soil rich in organic matter. Gardenias need fussing over in the form of supplemental feeding with an iron-rich, acidic fertilizer.

■ *Sarcococca hookerana* var. *humilis* / Sweet box
Midspring
Zone 6
Sweet box, a ground-cover member of the boxwood family, grows 18 inches high and spreads to cover a wide area. The leaves are deep glossy green. Tiny white flowers form in clusters and emit a honeylike fragrance in late winter. Plant in rich, well-drained soil in full or partial shade. If you loosen the soil and amend it with organic matter, it will spread more quickly.

Fragrant Perennials

■ *Convallaria majalis* / Lily-of-the-valley
Spring
Zone 2
Lily-of-the-valley is a deciduous ground cover with upright medium green leaves turning yellow in fall. The foliage forms a thick mat. The very fragrant, white bell-like flowers are suspended from stalks and bloom for two weeks in midspring. Plant in part sun or shade in any soil. It is vigorous.

■ *Lilium* species and hybrids / Lilies
Summer
Zone 4
These popular tall perennials with large flowers are available in a marvelous variety of height (2 to 6 feet), flower color (whites, pastels, pink, lavender, and freckled), and time of bloom (April to September). Fragrant types include the Madonna lily *(L. candidum);* regal lily *(L. regale),* and the many Oriental hybrids. Lilies like full sun with some afternoon shade. The soil must be well drained. Thoroughly work in compost or peat moss to a depth of 12 inches.

■ *Narcissus jonquilla* / Jonquils, Daffodils
Spring
Zone 4
Everybody knows daffodils, but not everybody knows and grows the fragrant cultivars of this very popular spring flower, which come in a variety of colors, sizes, heights, and times of bloom. The golden yellow jonquil 'Trevithian' blooms in midspring; the poeticus, or pheasant-eye type, 'Actea', blooms at the end of the season. Fragrance is usually noted in garden center literature or mail-order descriptions. Plant daffodils in any soil in full or part sun. Good drainage is essential.

■ *Paeonia* hybrids / Peony
Spring
Zone 3
A great, luscious-flowered fragrant perennial, peonies produce a mound of deep green foliage 2½ feet tall and wide. In late May and early June the 4- to 8-inch-wide flowers open atop long stems. Choose from hundreds of cultivars with colors ranging from white to pink to rose to deep red. The handsome foliage turns maroon to bronze in fall before dying back. Plant in full sun in well-drained, fertile soil, preferably neutral in pH. Amend the soil deeply with organic matter, such as leaf mold or peat moss.

■ *Phlox paniculata* / Garden phlox
Summer
Zone 3
Between July and September, garden phlox lifts domes of colorful, fragrant flowers to heights of 24 to 40 inches. Colors range from pure white to pink, red, rose, and lilac. Garden phlox forms clumps that steadily expand. It is happy

Tropical angel's trumpet (Brugmansia *sp.*) *drapes a classical statue with coarse foliage and a musky fragrance to create a garden corner with mysterious allure.*

in fertile soil with lots of organic matter. Good drainage is a must. Powdery mildew can be a problem in humid summers; excellent cultivars that are mildew resistant are available.

Fragrant Annuals

- *Nicotiana* species / Flowering tobacco
  Full sun
  The elongated, trumpet-shaped flowers are most fragrant at night, so plant nicotianas near the patio. Flower colors include white, pink, red, and green. Leaves stay low; flower stalks reach to 3 feet. Plant bedding plants or sow seed directly in the garden after danger of frost.

■ *Matthiola incana* / Stock
Spring
Full sun

The very fragrant lilac, pink, red, or white flowers grow on stalks reaching about 2 feet tall. Stock grows best where spring temperatures are cool. Sow seed directly in fertile soil.

■ *Petunia* × *hybrida* / Hybrid petunia
Full sun

These bedding plants have large, profuse, cheery flowers that last through the heat of summer. The color range is wide. Fragrance may be more pronounced at night. Plant bedding plants in average soil.

A FEW FAVORED PERENNIALS

Nurseries are jammed with perennials each spring, and, of course, all of us shop with our eyes. Perennials are the subject of many wonderful books, but here are a few durable, dependable types that will make any garden better. Combine these plants with some of the fragrant perennials and a ground cover, and you will have a great start for a tremendous-looking small-space garden.

■ *Coreopsis grandiflora* / Coreopsis
Summer
Zone 5

This sassy, bright yellow, daisy-flowered border plant is easy to grow and plentiful with bloom. The cultivar 'Sunray' hoists double yellow flowers atop 18-inch stems. Coreopsis is not particular about soil; it does well in hot, dry locations or in reflected heat. Thread-leaf coreopsis *(C. verticillata)* has finely cut leaves and forms a delicate-looking mound showered with yellow daisy flowers in midsummer. It must have full sun.

■ *Gaura lindheimeri* / Gaura
Summer
Zone 5

Gaura has wandlike airy stems, but it is barbed-wire tough. From midspring to the first hard frost, this sturdy Texas native lifts reddish stems covered in star-shaped flowers as high as 5 feet, but it can be easily managed at half that height.

Bees landing on the flowers tip the stems like pendulums. This tap-rooted plant is happy in any soil, sun to shade, and is drought resistant.

- *Helleborus orientalis* / Lenten rose
  Early spring
  Zone 4

  Lenten rose blooms from January to April, depending on the climate zone. The cup-shaped flowers, 2 to 3 inches across, form nodding clusters in shades of white, pink and maroon on stems approximately 1 foot high. The coarse-textured, glossy, evergreen foliage forms a mound reaching 18 inches tall and wide. Plant Lenten rose in any well-drained soil in partial sun to shade.

- *Hemerocallis* species / Daylily
  Summer
  Zone 3

  Yes, each flower lasts only a day, but the plants are in bloom for about three weeks. Daylilies are very hardy and come in an astonishing variety of colors. The flowers appear on branched scapes rising 1 to 6 feet tall in early, mid, or late summer. 'Stella d'Oro', a shorter selection, flowers continuously all summer. Coordinate the height and time of bloom with other perennials. Locate in full sun or light shade in well-worked soil. One of the easiest plants to grow.

- *Iris sibirica* / Siberian iris
  Spring
  Zone 4

  Siberian iris is one of the best of this wonderful group of perennials. The narrow, grasslike foliage reaches 2 to 3 feet tall. The delicate, plentiful flowers are borne several to a stalk in midspring. The colors range from purple and deep blue to white. Plants grow in widening clumps. Plant in full sun or part shade. Siberians prefer moist soil but will grow very well in ordinary soil. Easy to grow and a nice choice for small spaces. There are short cultivars as well.

- *Lobelia cardinalis* / Cardinal flower
  Late summer
  Zone 2

  A native plant of lightly shaded, moist sites, cardinal flower produces handsome spikes of deep red 1½-inch flowers. The lowest flowers on the spikes open first, and the entire show may continue from late summer to early fall.

The plant has an upright form and good-looking foliage. Plant in wet or moist soil in partial sun to shade.

■ *Pennisetum alopecuroides* / Fountain grass
  Summer to fall
  Zone 5
  Fountain grass, one of the best of the ornamental grasses, grows into a handsome, wispy clump of thin, fine leaves about 3 feet tall and wide. The feathery flower spikes appear in midsummer and last into fall as the foliage turns a warm tan or golden color. Blends well with many plants as a backdrop or accent. Plant in full to partial sun in any soil.

■ *Rudbeckia fulgida* 'Goldsturm' / Black-eyed Susan
  Summer
  Zone 3
  This is the classic golden yellow daisy with the dark brown disk in the center. The plant grows approximately 24 inches tall and wide, sometimes larger. The coarse foliage is deep green. Flowers are profuse and last from midsummer through fall. Rudbeckia combines well with many other flowers. Plant in ordinary soil in full sun. Water it when the leaves droop.

■ *Sedum hybrida* 'Autumn Joy' / Autumn Joy sedum
  Summer
  Zone 3
  This sedum grows in a clump 2 to 3 feet tall and just about as wide. The clusters of tiny flowers form a rounded crown on top of sturdy small stems. The flowers open pink in late summer and darken to deep rust by fall before they dry. This is broccoli, bronze and beautiful. Plant in full sun in any soil. Autumn Joy is very drought resistant.

HARDINESS ZONE MAP

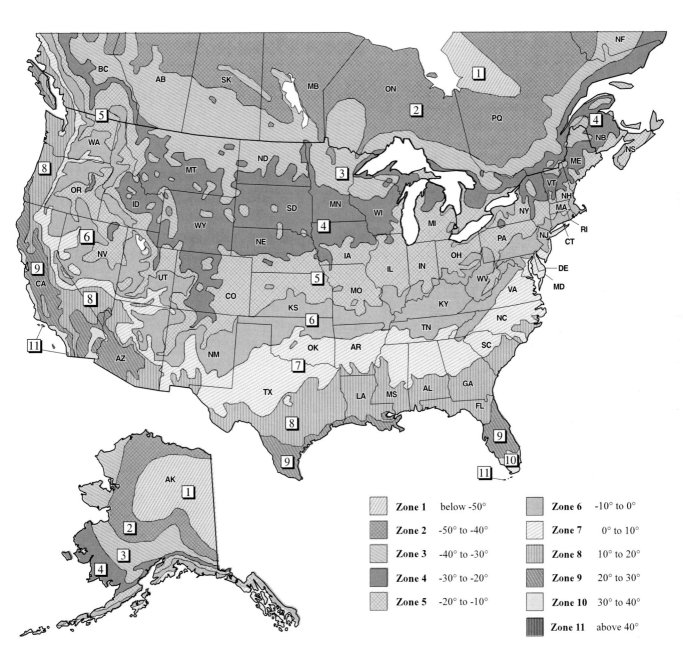

Zone 1	below -50°	**Zone 6**	-10° to 0°
Zone 2	-50° to -40°	**Zone 7**	0° to 10°
Zone 3	-40° to -30°	**Zone 8**	10° to 20°
Zone 4	-30° to -20°	**Zone 9**	20° to 30°
Zone 5	-20° to -10°	**Zone 10**	30° to 40°
		Zone 11	above 40°

PHOTO CREDITS

Karen Bussolini: 8 top (Sharon Mann, designer)

R. Todd Davis: 36, 42

Derek Fell: 3, 4, 7, 11, 12, 13, 17, 20, 24 top, 24 bottom, 27, 28, 29, 31 top, 31 bottom, 33, 38 top, 38 bottom, 41, 44, 45, 47, 49, 50, 52, 55, 56, 59, 61, 62, 63, 65, 67, 71, 72, 75, 76, 77, 78, 90, 102, 111, back cover

Charles Marden Fitch: 19

Charles Mann: iii, 8 bottom, 14, 23

Steve Silk/*Fine Gardening*: vi–1, 80

Linda Yang: 43

INDEX

Page numbers in italics refer to illustrations.

Titles available in the Taylor's Weekend Gardening Guides series:

Organic Pest and Disease Control
Safe and Easy Lawn Care
Window Boxes
Attracting Birds and Butterflies
Water Gardens
Easy, Practical Pruning
The Winter Garden
Backyard Building Projects
Indoor Gardens
Plants for Problem Places
Soil and Composting
Kitchen Gardens
Garden Paths
Easy Plant Propagation
Small Gardens
Fragrant Gardens
Topiaries and Espaliers

At your bookstore or by calling 1-800-225-3362